# Richard Meltzer's
## *Gulcher*

"*Gulcher* ... should have brought him
attention from mainstream critics that Hunter Thompson
received with *Fear and Loathing in Los Vegas*."
> —Ken Tucker, *L.A. Herald Examiner*

"Meltzer was 'there,' in '65-'68, a receptive cognizant
participant in a moment that jumpstarted many a mental
Volkswagen. It seemed like a good thing at the time, and
Meltzer, along with Lester Bangs and sometimes Nick Tosches,
provided its most durable musical reportage while it lasted."
> —Richard Gehr, *Village Voice*

"There is a line of thought that every culture gets the critic it
deserves. Richard Meltzer is living proof of the validity of that
line of thought. *Gulcher* was the book that brought that to the
world's attention. How very unfortunate for some of the Great
Pretenders lurking around that it's back in print again."
> —Ed Ward

"Richard Meltzer is a Renaissance man who has written lyrics
for Blue Oyster Cult as well as reams of inspiring gonzoid
criticism covering everything from boxing to food. Not for the
squeamish, Meltzer is a man with a dirty mind and a pure
heart, and the two collide to wonderful effect in his writing."
> —Kristine McKenna, *Los Angeles Times*

"Richard Meltzer has been our brave and faithful culture scout
for twenty years, and all it's gotten him is notoriety. It's time
we made him rich and famous. He's funny, he's smart, he's mad
as hell and he always gets even."
> —Michael Herr, author of *Dispatches*

"A gonzo H.L. Mencken, a Kerouacish motormouth with Terry
Southernish flair for satiric demolition."
> —*Booklist*

"Rock writing is dying. But it's not a case of murder. It's a case of blatant suicide. Boring writers and condescending magazines are destroying a music and lifestyle that previously had enough energy to sustain itself despite such hardships. Perhaps the problem is that rock has been looked upon as an art-form for too long....But two things have outlasted five years of serious rock writing. The fact that rock and roll is not an art-form (it's a comedy show) and that rock and roll is just not good music (it's a bunch of tasteless crap).

"But rock and roll is bad on purpose. You have to look at it from the viewpoint of the typical teenager. It takes ten minutes to write bad music and ten years to write good music. So if you love music and have a desire to perform it, why the fuck should you waste all that time learning technique? Fuck all the fundamentals and fuck all the formalities. Just play the music....

"That's Richard Meltzer's strong point in *Gulcher*. This is the first book written about rock and roll that isn't analytical, biographical, historical or made for reference....The real coup of the book is the fact that someone has come out in the straight press and said that sports, drugs, sex, booze, television, sex, wrestling, obnoxiousness, and sex have as much to do with ruckenrull as any of the loud stuff they call music. It's been an undeniable fact of life for a long time but nobody has had the balls to say it. Probably scared they would be called silly or dilettante, many critics simply didn't incorporate their lifestyles into their writing. Well it's out in the open now and I predict the day will come when *CREEM* will keep the heading 'America's Only Rock and Roll Magazine' and not have one article on music.

"This isn't a book you read once and put up on the shelf to collect dust with the other classics. You're going to read it over and over again. And I don't mean you are going to read it once and then refer to it a month later. I mean you are going to read a chapter and then read it over and over and over again until you either understand it or memorize it.

"So how about it, gang? Why don't we all get together and try and save rock writing. Boycott all pretentious, analytical bullshit and get down to some good old rock and roll entertainment. Come join the under-the-counter culture."

—Andy Shernoff, *Creem*

"Legendary.... Hits, misses, excesses and all, Meltzer is a real original: a one-of-a-kind writer who rarely lacks something to say and usually finds his own best way to say it."

—*L.A. Daily News*

"[Richard Meltzer] is a critic of perception."

—Joe Franklin

"Meltzer's writing is from-the-hip and off-the-top-of-the-head.... He sidetracks, but rarely derails. Comparisons to gonzo scribe Hunter S. Thompson and Charles Bukowski have been made, and made aptly. So too, to greater and lesser degree, William S. Burroughs (raw sex), Tom Wolfe (keen social observation) and Timothy Leary (frayed synapses).... In his own twisted, irascible, irrational way, Richard Meltzer makes a lot of sense."

—*Philadelphia Inquirer*

"Richard Meltzer and the mule of his brilliance harrow rings around most of what passes in these post-literate days for writing, wisdom, and wit. A joy and revelation, his is a *Phaedo* to which Lou Costello has brought the lasagne."

—Nick Tosches

# GULCHER

Post-Rock Cultural Pluralism in America
(1649–1993)

# Richard Meltzer

CITADEL UNDERGROUND
Citadel Press
Published by Carol Publishing Group
New York

CITADEL UNDERGROUND

First Citadel Underground Edition, October 1990

Copyright © 1972, 1990 by Richard Meltzer
Introduction copyright © 1972 by Lester Bangs

A Citadel Press Book
Published by Carol Publishing Group

Editorial Offices
600 Madison Avenue
New York, NY 10022

Sales & Distribution Offices
120 Enterprise Avenue
Secaucus, NJ 07094

In Canada: Musson Book Company
A division of General Publishing Co. Limited
Don Mills, Ontario

Manufactured in the United States of America
ISBN 0-8065-1197-4

Originally published in 1972 by Straight Arrow Publishers, San Francisco.
This edition published by arrangement with the author.

This time, for Donald Goodman,
Don Goodman, Dr. Don Goodman
(he taught me well).

# Contents

# Introduction to the Citadel Underground Edition

There are few things more annoying than artists' mutual-p.r. societies. You know the story: a pack of self-proclaimed geniuses band together to acknowledge each others' skills and provide the needed hype at the proper time. It's a supreme exercise in mutual masturbation, and it currently flourishes nowhere more prominently than in the New York pop scene.

Richard Meltzer is from New York, both physically and to the core of his spirit. I seriously doubt if he could live anywhere else. In the course of his career he has received his share of hype from friends and VIP's of assorted sleazoid stripes in that scene, although he has run afoul of the New York cultural Mafia on more than one occasion too.

I should also mention that he is a personal friend of mine, so this may seem as incestuous as the rest. Except that I was a Meltzer fan before I was a Meltzer drinking *confrère*, and if you're lucky enough to meet him and have ever been a fan you'll discover that the personae expressed on the page and in the person are very close to one another and form, in fact, a brilliantly unified whole. You read Meltzer like you spend a couple of hours at a bar every once in a while with an old friend who also happens to be a great *raconteur*. The subject can be anything, because it's the *style* that hooks you.

We live in a time when contemporary literature has rotted to the point that seemingly any creep with good vibes, a soul to shill, and minimal verbal facility can win himself a readership so solipsistically faithful that, why, just like any popstar, he can turn out the most vapid dreck imaginable and they'll love it every time.

Meltzer is one of the few young writers to emerge as an alternative to that. While every first book joker hitchhiking between Berkeley and Cambridge as he records his impressions is busy taking himself so seriously, not to mention self-consciously, as to be insufferable, and while seemingly every "counterculture" writer seems to feel that he would be playing hooky if for a single second he stopped reminding us of how oppressed he is, how deep is his empathy with the Third World and the sexually oppressed, how much he hates the war, how many tears he sheds over his brothers and sisters in every hovel from the Boardwalk to Tijuana—while all this neo-Calvinist flapdoodle is going on, Meltzer refreshes by totally ignoring or at best gently mocking the sanctimonies of his peers. He doesn't even bother attacking the Youth Shuck, but settles instead for wandering randomly with an easy, conversational style and an eye almost childlike in its basic lucidity through the entire spectrum of our Disposall culture, picking up artifacts and anecdotes he finds along the way and reporting them with absolute glee and with consistent attention to details any other writer would miss.

*Gulcher* is doubtless the most unique work on the, uh, culture that we're surrounded with to appear yet in the '70's, and part of its uniqueness lies in the fact that Meltzer is interested in absolutely *everything*. He'll write about things like bubble gum cards with the same interest and flair he applies to moon shots, and, no matter how mundane the subject matter, he always manages to make the discursion interesting, revelatory, humorous, and *fun* all the way.

According to Meltzer, this book came about when he was approached by *Rolling Stone*'s new Straight Arrow Press (which apparently had been somewhat impressed by his rep even though I'll bet money that they still don't know what he or this volume are about), and was asked to write a book for them.

"What on?" Meltzer asked.

"Culture," they replied.

"Oh, yeah, that stuff," said Richard. So, after pocketing the advance, he set over the next few months to the task of compiling this compendium of psychic hubcaps on the contemporary scene. He claims now that it's all a bunch of shit, and I know people who watched him write specific chapters for this volume just to pass the time while drunk at their houses, but the facts are that, in spite of an incredible diversity of subject matter the book really hangs together, and it contains an awful lot of the best stuff Meltzer's ever done.

The title is a dead giveaway both to the book's unity and to Meltzer's own demoliton of all pretensions through absolute parody of them. *Gulcher* is a brilliant coinage describing what you get on the last frontier of culture: not the old familiar culture that *Time* and *Saturday Review* and every other rag wrings week after week, nor the by-now deadeningly puerile "counterculture" that has had more books published about it in the past eight months than any other movement of equivalent insignificance in all of human history.

What Richard Meltzer is onto is what he calls "the under-the-counter culture," which is in a large part so humble or commonplace that it's usually overlooked. Even though, as he proves in this book without ever coming right out and saying it, the under-the-counter culture says at least as much about America as any of its more weighty cousins.

A listing of some of the topics and chapter titles from this book should begin to give you some example of which counter Meltzer is under:

The Top Ten Boxers as compiled by *Ring* magazine; Japanese monster movies; wallets, their functionalism and what and where are the best ones; "Marianne Is Faithful," wherein Meltzer finds an unmailed letter from a stranger to another stranger in the street, reads and sets it down for us, and concludes that it's actually from and about people we all know very well, except that we don't really know these other people any better than we know the two strangers who never mailed or received the letter, except that in fact we know those two strangers far better, so . . . except that Meltzer would never stoop to stating it so obviously; "Not All Rubbers Are Dubbers"—prophylactics; "A Fatal Jerkoff on the Moon"; bowling; Rocky Graziano's struggle to become a TV star, complete with Meltzer's list of ideas for story pilots ("13. A hypochondriac who gets a different fake disease every week"); "The Wonderful World of Booze"; a contest between the Luckies and Camels packs for aesthetic supremacy among cigarettes; a review of a book about famous excecutions of history (" . . . the first electric chair electrocution . . they didn't have any idea of how much juice to pump into the poor sucker so they really baked him to a crisp! His brain was as hard as a brick when they took it out and his face was reddish purple, and there was lots of froth and well-done meat! A lot like that similar scene in *Catcher in the Rye*"); football; tit shots in pre-Comics Code Authority comic books; the relationship between stamp collecting and the drug culture; bottlecap collecting; a consumer guide to tampons and sanitary napkins; a consumer report on M&M's candy; public dress mores in the age of the Wide Open Tits; the influence of Ogden Nash on Allen Ginsberg; a report on various snuffs and their audience; a report on brands of cigars and their audience; the state of beards today; plastic robots and other Xmas toys; Waylon Jennings' hairline; going fishing without worrying if it's hip anymore or not; a report on toilet paper; the Roller Derby; hydrophobia at Disneyland; "Neil Sedaka: Horseman of the Apocalypse"; the caging of animals in TV children's shows (ending with "FREE ALL ANIMAL PRISIONERS! POWER TO THE PACHYDERMS!"); the Sickle Cell Anemia Telethon; etc.

Some of those subjects may be written about all the time, but Meltzer's perspective is always so unique that you treasure his observations, even about things like football. And where else are you going to find in-depth consideration of snuff, bottlecap collecting, the relative quality of asswipes and Kotexes, and the packaging of Luckies and Camels? Nobody else but Meltzer would write about subjects like these, and certainly nobody could actually make it work, sustain it, and entertain us so thoroughly in the process.

The title is as good a joke as the preface "by Blaise Cendrars," sent all the way from Paris especially for this volume and the first thing old Blaise has wrote in many a year, so you know he's mightily impressed by this new kid. Calling the book *Post-Rock Cultural Pluralism in America (1649-1993)* is at once a throwback to Meltzer's own academic background which he has shed since it made his first book (*The Aesthetics of Rock*) mostly unreadable, and it is a pie in the face to all the academic pretensions in this culture, our culture, because it's like trying to analyze a hamburger for what makes pubes live on 'em and hang around the stand all day and night. It's like trying to tell a stranger about rock 'n' roll. You can bet *Gulcher* won't be featured in too many university courses: it's too alive.

And you can also bet that every bit of this, down to the last report on some has-been tank fighter's old sweatsox, has something to do with rock 'n' roll. Much more, in fact, than the mullings in the weighty tomes of rock critics who endlessly sift and analyze the music, searching for literary/social significance and sonic parallelism. Because rock 'n' roll ain't supposed to be artistically and socially significant; as Adny Shernoff of *Teenage Wasteland Gazette* says, it's supposed to be crass trash which stands outside your moralities and aesthetics, as its own kicks, and it doesn't have to mean a damn thing.

The miracle of Meltzer is that he doesn't have to either. You can enjoy him even when it's obvious that he doesn't know where he's going himself. (Some carpers have claimed that none of his stuff means anything, but they're also usually the kind of people who would complain about the lack of thematic subtlety in "Wop bop a loo bop a lop bam boom!") And yet, at the same time, it becomes apparent—if you want it to—that most of these pieces have more levels than the surface on which they so buoyantly entertain. They are as significant as any writing being done today because they are about our lives and how we live them: they perform the magical feat of taking precisely what we take for granted and opening it up to us as richly and revealingly as anything more obviously "meaningful."

So Meltzer's no dadaist as some have supposed. He's a humanist disguised as a lurching drunken juvenile delinquent at play in the rubble of civilization (as his publisher has condescendingly hyped him). But then, they also claim in their blurb that he's a "dope crazed ... maniac," when he is nothing of the kind, although I guess you still gotta have a password if you want in the club. With Meltzer the password is fun, and his club and beat are every unostentatious bloom of life in the world that catches his eye. Don't miss him.

Lester Bangs

(This introduction originally appeared as a review of *Gulcher's* original edition in *Coast* magazine, November, 1972.)

# Peripheral Pumice: A Preface
# by Blaise Cendrars

For some reason people still read books and mags that don't have pictures. The structure they've been fed of late has tended towards the delineation of youth culture as meaning-laden and quality-oriented. This is indeed strange for a culture whose cutting edge has begun and ended with rock and roll, crucial for its collapse of such dichotomies as the trivial and the awesome, the relevant and the irrelevant, the interesting and the boring, the topical and the eternal, the polar and the continuous, the     and the     . Recent cultural hierarchies have cut off a large mass of ongoing objects and events from the mainstream of the officially contemporary. These items remain and sometimes even flourish but are no longer mainstream, or they are banished or ignored as if they never were, the apparent reason being that no hip web remains for joining all (or even most or many) of them together in any journalistically palatable non-selfconscious conglomerate. In this process rock itself has disappeared as the true revolutionary force it once was, altered into a merely meaningful form of merely official mainstream importance.

Since rock itself no longer remains as a true forefront the time has come for the elevation of those other cultural elements easily meriting as much public concern and in many instances already out of the background and simply not yet covered in writing to the point of neutralization or negation by critical hacks and overexposure. What it's time for even more is the playing out of *all* cultural gimcracks on a general level before the next big specific single focal point achieves the insipid overplay of hierarchical priority: time to run through the gamut of booze, television, sports, Hollywood, etc. before any single one of them achieves a self-defeating prominence as was afforded rock and roll (the *Village Voice* and *Rolling Stone* have already cottoned to sports, for instance). In so doing, these widely varied channels of contextual experience will remain potent in their bland semi-obscurity on the periphery of culture even if and when outbreaks of monism should arise.

After all, no pluralism is tactically possible without a view of the gross absurdity advanced by the elevation of a particular *one* out of a particular *many*, nor is it possible without this initial world construction, for with an equivalence of levels within the culture for any and all possible and actual objects a monism already exists which is almost impossible to shake during any given finite span of time. Hence: pluralism *requires* mainstream and periphery as distinctly separate domains despite whatever objects any given creator, spokesman, audience or entrepreneur might place within the dichotomy. And if eruptions of monism are so prevalent, an eruption of honest-to-goodness pluralism is bound to pop up sooner or later. Meltzer can dig it, just watch him.

*Paris, 1972*

# Gulcher

Culture is a vulture but there's also vulture culture and cultured vultures and cultured yogurt (cherry, peach, pear, pineapple, grape, vanilla, plain, cherry vanilla, pineapple orange, cranberry orange, mandarin orange, coffee, apricot, raspberry, blueberry, boysenberry, prune). And speaking of vulture culture there's counter-culture and under-the-counter culture too. But whether you call it kulture with a k or kulchur with a k and a ch and without the e it's still the same thing and you can't disguise it with pretty frills and a gallon of dogsweat. It still has two syllables and TWO-SYLLABLE WORDS SUCK so you can just forget it, man. It's no fun at all and even fun wouldn't be fun if it was called funjure or funion or funching. But somehow fucking is still loads of fun even though there's that extra 3-letter cluster of vowels and consonants. Proof positive that there are exceptions everywhere you look. But don't look too hard, you might get eyestrain!

# Who Invented the Top Ten?

Hey Buster who invented the top ten? Who's the first guy to ever do it? Come on man, *who?* Could it have been Matthew Arnold? Um, could it be Herbert Marshall? Herbert Marcuse? Peter Van Eyck? Meister Eckhardt? Dwayne Hickman? Ray Milland? John Dewey? Harold Zyskind? Leo Tolstoy? Bunny Berrigan? Rastis Coker? William H. Taft? Jerry Wexler? Monty Montgomery? Cardinal Richelieu? Symphony Sid? Abigail Folger? Alan Freed? Alan Hale? Nathan Hale?

No but that's pretty close cause it was another Nathan, Mr. Nat Fleischer. But this is only one of those *most likely type things*, it's only most likely that it was him, don't stake your immortal soul on it. Most likely it was Nat Fleischer of CUNY class of early 20th century. He got his degree in botany and he helped raise plants for World War II.

Well Walter Camp if that's his name had the first all-American football thing even before Nat was out of his diaper. And football has eleven guys on a team so that was a top eleven. But they didn't number the guys. Oh yeah they numbered the guys on their jerseys so you could tell them with a scorecard but Walter himself didn't number them. He only listed them by position, there wasn't any kind of hierarchy except maybe whichever position he listed first or if he listed it from left to right or anything like that. Whatever it was didn't have numbers and even if you counted in your head it was still eleven and not ten.

Okay so somewhere during the 20's Nat started this thing called *The Ring—Ring* magazine for short—and it's still the best magazine in the world today bar none. It's got complete covereage of every fight that took place in every obscure outpost of a fight town in the whole world during the month. Bruce Trampler covers Columbus, Ohio for them and Gillie Campbell does Kingston, Jamaica. Nat Fleischer's probably the one single person most responsible for the dullardliness of boxing today but he was once strictly okay. That was when he was just starting out and he decided to be the sole rater of boxing for the whole world and he was. He started doing the top ten for every division from flyweight on up to heavyweight. He even decided to acknowledge the junior lightweight and junior welterweight divisons when he realized it could only mean more fun with figures. But the figures have always been 1 through 10. Except in his annual end-of-the-year edition which has millions of guys rated with numbers and letters and all sorts of stuff but that's only one month out of twelve. He's always been a master at crystallizing things into his little system and only recently has he been revealed to be the cretin he is.

Well anyway in *On the Waterfront* there's that scene where Marlon Brando is in the car with his brother Rod Steiger and he says to Rod "I coulda been a con-*ten*-duh" and by that he means that he coulda been in the top ten of *Ring* magazine for a lengthy stay and that's all he means by that. Oh he means a lot of stuff but that's what it's in terms of, just that and no more. Nat Fleischer. He's talking in that scene about Nat Fleischer so do you realize how powerful Nat Fleischer is?

Like Nat's main claim to fame has always been the fact that he's rated Jack Johnson the number one heavyweight of all time. He probably even saw Jack Johnson way back in those days and not too many other alive people did who are still alive. He not only saw him but he liked what he saw. It was a real intelligent move to put Jack up there, it was a real acknowledgment of just how hip he was to boxing innovation cause he really once was. Like all boxing has ever been has been a heap of complaints about how things have been shit since Marciano retired. Or since Joe Louis. Or Jack Dempsey. Y'know like it's always the big vain search for yesterday and it goes all the way back to John L. Sullivan.

Now there's probably fewer than ten thousand people total who ever saw Sullivan fight in all his fights put together and yet somehow he was the first to get real 20th century type sports hype so they decided to start things out with him. Marquess of Queensberry and padded gloves and stuff like that was just the excuse for calling him against Jim Corbett the first official actual heavyweight title fight. And he lost it in fact and then he retired to hogfat and when you get down to it he was probably as worthless as Mickey Mantle. But it wasn't until Jim Jeffries came along that people thought well maybe here was another John L.

Okay so he retires and sooner or later there's this scrawny creep going around claiming the title called Tommy Burns. He's no John L., he's no Jim Jeffries, he's no Bob Fitzsimmons, he's no Jim Corbett and he isn't even a Marvin Hart who had the title somewhere in there too. He's the worst shit to come down the pike since the beginning of the whole show and it's already in through the first decade of the twentieth century and what the fuck's the fight populace to do?

Okay so into this whole dismal piss bucket comes Jack Johnson, who not only can beat the living shit out of Tommy Burns but who also happens to be the REAL ACTUAL AUTHENTIC REAL LIFE JOHN L. SULLIVAN. Plus the fact that he's black so he's not only hitting the sports nail on the head but he's everything quality like that is not allowed to be embodied in. He's also the most awesome display of *defensive* boxing anybody's ever seen and what the goddam sonofabitch is boxing supposed to be if not the *manly art of self-defense*? He's so good he can toy with anybody, make anybody look silly. He's the real thing as real as it's ever been and he's living out every potential it's ever had and the country wants him dead cause he's black.

Okay and so Nat Fleischer actually knew how important Jack Johnson was and so you'd figure that would set him up pretty good as far as not being a racist goes but that was way before the advent of the first real innovator since Jack Johnson himself. Muhammad Ali who Fleischer detests even more vehemently than the guys did back in the days of the White Hope Era. Cause Fleischer's beef is on aesthetic grounds. He just can't cope with the man on aesthetic grounds and so he's had to enlist the support of all sorts of spurious ethical shit that he doesn't even believe in (for instance did you know that the cover story on the welcome-home-veterans issue following WW2 was Rocky Graziano who *deserted* during wartime?) to rally support for his anti-Ali campaign. Like he was pissed off at veterans groups for not protesting New York State's granting of a license to him for the Frazier fight and like what the fuck's he talking about?

Well anyway there's more to the story of Jeffries and Johnson besides the fact that they were the first two bonafide John L's. Johnson finally tracked down Tommy Burns in Australia and beat his ass so bad the cops had to stop it and then he went on to beat everybody around except for the guys he wouldn't fight either like Sam Langford but that's another story. Okay so they get Stanley Ketchel to try to wrest the title from his hands and Ketchel's only a middleweight. Before the fight there's some sort of agreement that neither guy gets hurt and it goes the distance so all the writers can get controversial about the outcome. Well somewhere midway through it Ketchel suddenly decides he can win so he tags Johnson and Johnson goes down. Okay so he's on the mat and he realizes Stan's pulled a fast one on him and so he puts everything he got into his next punch and lands it as he's getting off the floor and it lands so hard it knocks Ketchel clear across the ring and that's that. So after that they finally had to convince poor old Jim Jeffries that he had to come out of retirement for his race and for the country as well. He's a real dipshit so he falls for it and he has to lose *99 pounds* to get in shape for the fight and they have the fight on the 4th of July and he gets clobbered as bad as it's ever been done and that's it for him and Johnson's still champ. Which suggests one strong possibility: if he hadn't done it, if he hadn't come out of retirement to try to be the true authentic white hope then maybe Fleischer would've rated him above Jack cause that way he would've been an undefeated guy and Johnson was his only loss. Cause Nat rates Jim number two so there's always the suspicion it would have been otherwise if he hadn't gotten his ass handed to him by Johnson.

I don't know, if you ever see Nat on the street you can ask him yourself but I don't particularly go for his list anyway and mine's a heck of a lot better:

1. Muhammad Ali
2. Jack Johnson
3. Jim Jeffries
4. Sonny Liston
5. Joe Louis
6. Jack Dempsey
7. Sam Langford
8. Rocky Marciano
9. Bob Fitzsimmons
10. Max Baer

The only reason Max Baer's on the list at all is he really beat Max Schmeling pretty good in the battle of the Maxes and he probably would've got beat even worse himself by Joe Frazier who would then take over as number 10 but Max B is dead and Max S is not so maybe Max S oughta be number 10 cause he's still alive and a fight with Frazier could be a possibility for some promoter who has some imagination. Dempsey's listed so low because he wasn't really much more than a slightly tougher Ingemar Johansson. He had a string of one-round knockouts going into his title fight with Willard (who was kind of an earlier Cleveland Williams) and who's ever gonna forget Ingo's one-round kayo over Eddie Machen and then the 3-round demoliton job he did on Patterson? Tunney was just a better Ezzard Charles so he doesn't count at all and Corbett never really did much except for the time he fought Joe Choynski on a boat and the fact that Choynski subsequently once beat Johnson in his early days or something like that. Like Corbett was a good boxer and he had a decent jab and all and Sullivan never really landed a single decent punch on him when they fought but the jab's sort of the embodiment of all that's dull about now. A jab at the beginning and a jab at the end are just about the same when you get down to what's palatable.

So the next time your pal tells you that "Brown Sugar" is number seven you really oughta look up your sleeve and grin to yourself about how numbers for things all started. Or maybe even recommend that he buy this book so he can learn himself. And as for Nat Fleischer, he maybe oughta either die or change his name to Flesher so he can star in the sequel to *Sins of the Fleshapoids*, cause he's not good for anything else. Hierarchies are ultimately self-something-or-other.

# The Second Greatest Double Feature of All Time

Yog was never in the Sino-Japanese War. Nor was Yog ever in the Russo-Japanese conflict. Nor was Yog even in the movie of the same name, *Yog—the Monster from Space*. Gazora was in that one and that's Gaz for short—and Zag backwards but that's still not Yog unless you change a couple letters and that's out of the question—so why'd they go and call it *Yog*? They being those Japo-Japanese filmmakers who made the film. But did they make the name too? Probably not and so it's named *Yog* in spite of itself. But shouldn't pictures have names of their own too, just like people and automobiles? Expecially *good* pictures, they deserve their own names more than bad pictures and *Yog*'s a good picture. If not the best.

Best in the West but maybe not the best in the East, but it's about a beast from the East. Well not exactly, there's also some shenanigans going on from space. And speaking of space there's many kinds. One is outer: that's taken care of in the movie by the strange blue light from the planet Jupiter that got into the satellite and ended up in the sea. That takes care of under space: the sea all around us and beneath our feet if we're in a boat or standing on a bridge. In Japan the only bridge that goes over the sea (rather than a lake or stream) is the Yokohama Bridge, designed in 1928 and survived the atomic blasts in nearby cities during the latter stages of WW2.

The blue stuff gets in the undersea monsters and makes them into very *big* monsters instead of just turtles and octopi which is what they started as. Then the giant octopus which has a man inside of it and he's a good actor, he walks the big rubber thing onto the land near the paper houses with a little bit of straw on them and then he stomps all over them and gets one of the villagers with his tentacle and the guy gets frostbite from it cause it's freezing cold. But frostbite and burns have similar symptoms but the guy's no simp so when he's getting married and he's in a stupor from having been attacked by the octopus he suddenly remembers that it was bats that chased the octopus away.

So they get some bats—and when was the last picture you saw where the bats were the good animals?—and they get them ready to make their unusual sounds when the giant sea crab comes along later. But how do the bats supposed to know that they're meant to *attack* the crab and the turtle? They don't which is exactly the point. Therefore the guys making the film employ something other than actual bats to go get em: they use animation in the way of large black specks against the sky. That can be an awful lot of work for the poor animators so the way they do it to make it easier is they do it perfectly symmetrical in the way of swarms of black specks up in the sky over the monsters. They use a mirror or a fold-over or something, however they do it is extremely skillful and exciting as the monsters go berserk and fall over the cliff to their deaths.

But that's not the end of it yet because the blue aura slips away from out of the corpses and gets into the real estate speculator with the funny neat little beard and the Ernie Kovacs composure. He gets took over but he doesn't completely succumb and so the humans can talk him into fighting the forces of outer space dedicated to destroying the human race on the planet earth. He staggers around and because it was the girl who told him and she has such lovely boobs under her shirt and brassiere but they still show thru he cannot turn her down and so he staggers around fighting the forces within him and then he falls against a two-dimensional palm tree. No it's not him falling into another world with crazy dimensions, it's just the filmmakers again experimenting with a new form of visual spectacular effect. Instead of using a 2-D backdrop with sky on it or something like that they use a 2-D *foreground* with palm trees on it and stuff like 3-D monstrosities in the background.

Eventually you get to see why it's an R-rated film. Before you do you keep wondering when the fornication's gonna start and with whom. Lots of chances for the romance to begin but it never does. The R comes in when the monsters are fighting at the end because the blue light has no control over them anymore. They fight and they fight and finally they get into a fighting position commonly regarded as sexual with both of them touching and white frothy material oozing around from an unknown source. But anybody old enough to be watching an R movie knows what the source is and so in the end everybody with a ticket is happy.

You know especially who's happy? The people who are students of classical Jap monster epics. Everything from the classics is contained in *Yog*: an island like in *Mothra* and all the other ones, a turtle like in that one about the turtle, double and triple causalities like in *The Mysterians*, men inside the costumes like in *Son of Godzilla*, praying around the fire like in *Godzilla vs. King Kong*, mountains like in *Rodan*, guys sacrificing their life like in *Godzilla*, airplanes and good music like in *Ghidra* and so on.

But it's just the teaser before the main event: *The Abominable Doctor Phibes*. Some people pronounce it fi-bees, some pronounce if f-eye-bz, but either way it's the finest Vincent Price movie ever made or produced. The reason is that never before has V. Price talked so little during the duration of any one single feature motion picture. In this one he has no face to talk with so he has to resort to some kind of gadget and he does that but not all the time. Because—let's face it—his voice stinks and the less the better. And his face stinks too but in this picture usually it's a mask of his face and not the real face so you don't have to see all his pimples with makeup on top of them to cover them up.

And when you get to see his real fake face underneath at the conclusion of *Dr. Phibes* it turns out to be a good one, even better than the one in *Doctor Sardonicus* with that frozen palsy thing that constricts his face (it wasn't Vin but it was somebody else just as good). But the best face in the whole picture—*Phibes* not *Sardonicus*—is the one that's been eaten up by grasshoppers. They were supposed to be locusts but locusts must cost too much or something and anyway the grasshoppers were big and just as ferocious. But as you all know there's no way you're going to get a grasshopper to just eat up a face without a little added incentive. That's cause they're normally vegetarians and vegetarians will never normally eat meat. That's a good idea. They should have carnivore restaurants with food disguised to look and taste like a vegetable, sort of like the converse of those protose steak abominations. Right, so the way they get the hoppers to eat the face is Phibes makes up a brew containing nothing but 100% brussels sprouts and he cooks them up into a green slime that also happens to be sticky as hell.

The stuff gets dripped onto her face from the floor above and they drill a hole around where her face is supposed to be. They don't do it around where her hole is supposed to be because this is not an R movie but a GP. It gets to cover up her face and—altho it is not discussed in the confines of the criminal investigation inside the movie—she may already be dead due to suffocation before the hoppers ever get there. But the hoppers do get there and their appetite is as big as a house. They eat the living shit out of her features and all that remains is bones and hair. But the hair resembles the head topping of an elderly individual so perhaps she aged in the grisly act of dying. That too is not discussed, rather it is left for after-movie discussions at such places as dining clubs and sewing circles.

Another discussion worth getting into is who was the Charlie Farrell who's mentioned in the credits at the beginning and who you don't know who he is when he shows up or even if he ever does show up at all. Could he be the Charlie Farrell who played Vernon Albright in *My Little Margie*? Could he be the Charles Farrell who played Margie's dad? The one who had Hillary Brooke for a girlfriend, the same Hillary Brooke who used to taunt Lou Costello all the time? Could he be that Charlie Farrell? Cause if he was the only person he could've been in the whole picture would be the guy who was in the bed in the very beginning who gets killed off right away. Unless of course Charlie Farrell was already dead, dead at somebody else's hands, maybe even the big fuckin killer in the sky.

But maybe he's still actually alive even though it wasn't him in *Dr. Phibes*. If so he could still be due to die real soon. And maybe it'll be rats that he dies due to. There are good rats in *Dr. Phibes* and they're even better than the rats in *Williard* and *Willard* is just generally dull anyway. There's nobody in it who is the world's greatest organ player such as Vincent Price playing the organ. He plays it with his hands going up in the air between strokes and Willard doesn't have any decent music at all. But *Dr. Phibes* has "Somewhere over the Rainbow" and "It's a quarter to three, nobody in the place except you and me" and it's well played by excellent musicians hidden somewhere while this fake robot band does the playing.

One sticky problem remains and that's how did that mask work that Phibes used to do in the guy at the party? It had a face like a frog but the thing in the back was different from most masks and it closed tighter and tighter by itself. Did it have a machine inside it? Another good thing about it was you couldn't tell the guy was dead until the blood dripped out because you couldn't see his face to see if he was still breathing or if his eyes were alive. And it saves actors that way because they don't have to play dead because the mask covers up their ham face gestures and they're lucky that way because if they did it wrong they'd get fired and they'd starve to death in oblivion.

Which is something that never happened to Lloyd Nolan, the star of one of the two that comprise *the* greatest double feature of all time. Both are about the sea and the one with Lloyd Nolan does not have Lloyd Bridges. He wears a frying pan over his face but you can still see his body clad in a white t-shirt on board the ship with a young lady. It's in black and white and the female lead is a Claudette Colbert look-alike. The sea does not rage outside the porthole but only just hangs in and the waves are extremely small. Yet it's not about the commercial sea-going fleet nor is it about the navy. Nor does he own the ship by himself, it's partly hers. It's not a comedy.

The other picture is totally forgot.

# Funktional

It sure as shootin ain't easy recording for Capitol Records, particularly if your music is all the colors of the rainbow. Which is of course the case with Grand Funk, known in a previous lifetime as Grand Funk Railroad. Planes are the way to fly so now they're just Grand Funk but there's more than train tracks in their way. Capitol labels for one thing. Back in the old days of the Beatles and Steve Miller and Quicksilver and Merle Haggard the labels on the records at Capitol were black with the Capitol dome and all the colors of the rainbow circumscribed thereupon somewhere in the vicinity. Whenever one of those platters got the spin from the turntable it was a full-color experience to go along with music—full color at no extra cost.

Well now it costs something extra when Capitol is involved. Full color has been abandoned in favor of—it hurts even to think about it—OLIVE GREEN! Ugh but that's not all, there's a hideously ugly logo thing up on top in purple. Ordinarily a great color if not in fact the greatest, but not even a good one here. It's in the shape of a "C" for Capitol stretched around a black image of a record with a fat white center! But that's not all: the purple thing overlaps a white inner outline of another "C" that happens to be superimposed on the repulsively vulgar olive green! Now everybody knows that olive and black don't go except when you're eating olives and they happen to be mixed green and black. But colors on records are worlds apart from colors on vegetables and fruits both with and without pits. Which all adds up to an uncompromisingly uncomfortable listening-and-watching experience when Capitol discs are involved.

And they're involved whenever Grand Funk non-bootlegs are filling the airwaves except when it happens to be a tape. But of course they've been able to overcome that, they walked up to the company president and the chairmen of the board and said quite plainly, "We'd like a change. No we don't want to leave Capitol, actually we're rather happy aboard the Capitol steamship. But we would like you to go and change the color of the label as a favor to us." And they did! It's now red, and although the purple's still there it looks like a *good* purple this time. Not the prettiest label in the world but not the ugliest either. Kind of like those old Nasco labels or Nasbro or whatever "Oh Julie" was recorded on. A nice vintage look. Now nobody's gonna turn off Grand Funk for visual reasons, not even hardened insensitive critics like Chuck Pulin.

Another problem is clothes. They do "Gimme Shelter" on the *Survival* album but what about "Gimme Clothing"? It's obviously on their mind because they're wearing all that caveman getup. Cavemen had to kill animals to wear clothing because they didn't know anything about plants yet. Now people know a lot about plants but they wear animal skins anyway.

But at least they don't use animal gut for their stringed instruments. That's an advantage of living during the Industrial Revolution, you're allowed to use metal strings and everybody's happy. And so's the sound, the sound's real good, in fact it's never been better. It's so good that it can fill Shea Stadium for $306,000. The price has gone up since the Beatles did it for only $304,000 but that's due to inflation. But they were smart in having only three guys in the band instead of four. $304,000 divided by 4 is only $76,000 but $306,000 divided by 3 is $102,000.00. That's of course before taxes. Taxes take a big bite out of your earnings but you can learn to live with it.

Mark Farner, Don Brewer and Mel Schacher have learned to live with that and more, including their parents. Anybody who can live with his parents and live to tell the tale has got to be superhuman. Supermen belong up in the sky and that's exactly where Grand Funk got put, up on that poster in Times Square, the flower of New York City. It was as high up in the air as buildings would allow, it could have been on the Empire State Building but the cost would have been prohibitive. In any event, when the poster came down there were tears in more eyes than one.

So now the only place you're gonna find billboards with the boys on them is Los Angeles, California, home of Capitol Records. Capitol puts posters on stuff like benches at bus stops, they really know how to do it up right. So it's no accident that these three titans of twang are on such a with-it label, after all they're with-it guys. What are they with? The apocalypse. And yet they are not self-destructive in any way, as the Doors were known to be. Morrison used to stick pins in his eyes when he got bored, or set his hair on fire. That can add up to rock and roll thrills and chills but it doesn't make for a long and productive career in music.

And Grand Funk is above all else *musical*. Music was meant to be played, listened to, and danced to, not necessarily in that order. But that's the way it always seems to be when Grand Funk is in town. How do they do it? Well first there's Mark on the guitar and vocals. Jazz people will tell you that a guitar is the equivalent of a saxophone and a trumpet, both crucial instruments within the domain of sound. One has improvisatory possibilities and the other is a cutting edge. Put them together and you've got a maelstrom of notes from heaven careening off the top of your head. The reason most guitarists like to sing too is the vibrations on their fingers set up vibrations in their bones and eventually their jaw. So they can't shut up. And besides, Mark is one of the top three or four vocalists in the world anyway, so why shouldn't he sing?

Then there's Mel on bass. If he wasn't playing you'd notice the discrepancy, believe you me! Bass is the link between rhythm and melody and without it you can kiss rock and roll goodbye. In the 1971 *Metronome* critics poll Mel finished second behind Andy Kulberg in the electric bass category (Doug Lubahn was third), a sign of the respect his playing has garnered for him of late. Ofttimes he will even take the lead while Mark loons back and croons a tune, proof that the lads are friends in addition to being stablemates.

Don's tubwork used to leave something to be desired, he was trying to do too many things at the same time. It turned out he was studying too many Grateful Dead records and as everybody knows they used to employ the two-drum formula for sure-fire success. Mark and Mel cornered him in earnest one day and told him to read the back of the album. He did and then immediately realized he had been trying to copy two drummers at once! Well from then on he's been satisfied to lay down a heavy beat and occasionally throw in an expertise-loaded drum roll for good measure.

Put them all together and you've got a fine kettle of fish, maybe the finest since 1961 (confidant Terry Knight, formerly of Terry Knight and the Pack of international renown, shares this belief). And you can't overrate the value of an audience. As Chester Burnett once said, "The men don't know but the little girls understand." And if all those hot foreheads breaking out into cold sweats are an indication, there's no telling how far these busters can go. Maybe even behind the Iron Curtain! Or Malagasy Republic! Or Latin America! It'll be a shame to see them go and let's hope they come back so they can save the world for us.

# A Tale of Three Cities

In this day and age of freedom from materiality wallets have become nearly extinct. Like who wants the size and shape of a dollar bill to determine the size and shape of the thing they're gonna keep their prized photos of the family in? And the horrible, heinous, repulsive, disgusting things are usually kept in a back pocket near the rectum, and you know what Norman Brown has to say about the relationship between filthy lucre and excrement.

But there is a ray of sunshine in the wallet controversy, and that's that they're being produced in plastic now. Which can only mean fewer dead animals now that leather's been given the heave-ho. And to heighten the advance these new wallets have made beyond the world of mere brutal stability is the fact of where you find them: airports. For people on the go-go-go.

San Francisco has a nifty line of dark blue plastic wallets with various scenes from around town on them. For instance, Chinatown. It even says it, "Chinatown." And there can't even be any confusion with New York's Chinatown because New York doesn't even have a Chinatown wallet. The only wallet they have is light blue, traditionally a girl's color since they must figure guys wouldn't go for it just yet, and it features lots of urban geography. Statue of Liberty, Empire State Building, La Guardia Airport, J.F.K. Int'l Airport, Rockefeller Center, United Nations Building, and—oops—Chinatown. Yeah, they do have New York's Chinatown on a wallet but it's not the greatest wallet in the world.

That honor belongs to the one on sale at the Miami airport with a map of Florida on one side and a photo of some oranges on the other. What's best about it is the map and the oranges are on a piece of paper that *may be removed and replaced by anything you want to display through the clear plastic backing.*

# Marianne Is Faithful

I found a letter, a well-written, informative letter, I found it in the street and there was no envelope. Maybe it had been read, maybe not. Perhaps it had been opened and then lost, perhaps it had even been stolen. But in all cases it should be passed on to the person for whom it was intended, at all costs, even the invasion of privacy. Had the letter been inside an open envelope I would have sealed it and mailed it on to the address written upon it; I would not have read it and if necessary I would have paid sufficient postage myself. Had I found it in sealed condition there would have been no problem and the receiver would never have known it had been tampered with in any way. But as there was no envelope and no address these questions are merely hypothetical and of no real value in helping this letter reach its destinaton.

There is a chance—however remote—that neither writer nor intended reader are up to this page in the book yet, in which case it is possible that even its printing herein will not assist the U.S. Mail. I would suggest that all Kates who know Mariannes, and vice versa, seriously consider the possibility that this letter involves them. Should you know a Kate or Marianne please do not hesitate to bring this to their immediate attention. As a further aid in identification no changes have been made in spelling as one's spelling is as personal as one's nose. Thank you for your care and cooperation.

June 25, 1970

Kate,

Received your letter the other day, I was so happy to hear about your boyfriend I sat down & cried I'm so happy for you! I hope it lasts for a long time. Don't worry about me knocking the shower bit, I think its beautiful. I'm glad your so honest with me, I feel now I can tell you what actually happened to me & George at his house that night we went to the Peanut House with Betty. Well, you might have guessed we had intercourse. Kathy I've never told anybody that; not even Rosemary. So I hope you'll keep it to yourself *forever*. It seems I can talk to you so much easier than anybody else. Because somehow I think you understand me. Oh, Kathy I wouldn't have done it if I didn't love him so much, and when I didn't see him for 3 months afterwards, I thought I had done the wrong thing. I'll never regret it, and I don't feel the least bit guilty.

His girlfriend is gone, I think I told you that when you were home. Well, last Wednesday Rosemary told me he was going to go to our graduation. Just knowing he was there, made me so happy. Afterwards I had all my friends over. I told Rose to ask him to come. Was I happy or what? when he walked in the door. In front of my parents & 20 kids he gave me a great big kiss after 3 months of not seeing him, then we went to another party. I had a fantastic night. Hes changed I know he cares for that girl very much. But I'm going to try everything I've got to get him back, and if that doesn't work I'll try some more until I give up. Thats all I can do! Any suggestions will gladly be listened too.

I think if its alright with with you I won't be able to get to New York until the end of Sept. or beginning of Oct, I'd love to make it sooner, but I'm working full time and with Chip's wedding there's all the showers & parties. I'm coming for sure however because I'm already starting to plan it! Can't wait!

Betty and I have been going out quite a bit lately. We went to Brunners, Pats, Gaslight East & Keystone 90's all within the last month. I'm getting quite tired of drinking however. The other night we rode our bikes to the Williamsville park & swang on the swings. Then we went out with Lynn & Janet one night. God what a night that was. First Lynn sang a love song to Janet, then they went for a walk together. It really got sickning after an hour or so.

Well, thats the exstent of whats knew here, can't wait to hear from you.

Until then have fun, & the hell with being good, hope everything works out for you!

Love ya,
*Marianne*

Jesus fuckin Christ I just realized it might be *Marianne Faithful!* Too much! All the clues are there, the George could be George

Harrison or George Martin and then there's the unnatural acts alluded to. The English are famous for their unnatural acts (Joe Meek of the Tornadoes—famous for their recording of "Telstar"— once killed himself on the anniversary of Buddy Holly's death because of an unhappy HOMOSEXUAL affair) and Marianne is supposed to have been in on the action with the Mars bar when Mick and Keith got busted that first time.

In fact even the opening sentence indicates that she wrote the letter. She talks about crying and after all her first hit was "As Tears Go By," wasn't it? Mick and Keith wrote it just for her and nobody believed it because people said it was such a dipshit song and she was such a wimp. But she sure looked sweet enough and soon enough the Stones recorded it themselves and not too long after that Mick was sweet on her. Sweet on her for a long time and rumour was he even paid for her divorce from some other guy after he was through with her. So she must be some boss chick.

She did lots of albums and occasionally she wore a tie on the cover but she never really got over her reputation of being an anemic Joan Baez. Sooner or latter Mary Hopkin came along and replaced her as the first lady of English song. But she was better because anemia is better than hogwash. She did the original version of "Sister Morphine" and I guess that's why Marianne's sick of drinking in the letter. Like after the hard stuff how's a body to go back to ethyl alcohol?

Does anybody know if Marianne was in town some time in the vicinity of two June 25's ago? If she was it couldn't have been for a concert because she's never done a live show in the U.S.A. Very few British broads ever do, the only one I can think of offhand is Julie Driscoll. I don't know, Cilla Black might have been but she doesn't really count. Another thing that doesn't count is the fact that Marianne was supposed to be in *Ned Kelly*, that putrid western that Mick made in Australia. She wasn't in it, she was getting sick at the time, on downs or something. But she was barely hot shit in all those Shakespearean things she did like *Hamlet* and *Midsummer Night's Dream*. Stuff like that's on television every once in a while and come to think of it she and Mick were on that show via satellite in 1967 with the Beatles recording "All You Need Is Love."

The *Thorndike Barnhart Handy Pocket Dictionary* defines *faithful* as "loyal; true; accurate." I don't know about the accurate but the loyal and true sums her up pretty good. What else but loyalty and truth would compel anybody to write to a moron like Kate? And she spells it with two L's anyway.

# Not All Rubbers Are Dubbers

Bags are cheaper than either an abortion, a wedding ring, pills, cancer treatments, tetracycline, penicillin or even coat hangers unless they're the free ones you get when you get your clothes back from the cleaners. Royal Knight prophylactics come two to the box for a quarter and they're cheap and you can get them in those dispensers in the bathrooms along the highways of certain states. Any budget can afford them and the packaging is elegant and it reminds you of the famous poem "In days of old when knights were bold and scumbags weren't invented they put a sock around their cock and babies were prevented." There's a knight in yellow and blue and they're manufactured by one of the most reputable firms in the world, Allied Latex of Dothan, Ala. Alabama's gift to the world and it's just sitting there begging to be unwrapped. So you don't mind if you do.

But to tell you true the box don't open easy. The box opens real easy but it's the cellophane on the outside you gotta reckon with first before you can get it out and onto your dick. (That's if you're a boy. If you're a girl it's still hard to get it out and up to your lips so you can blow it up like a balloon. And with the ever rising cost of balloons nowadays they're almost the thriftiest balloons in town and a great idea for junior's birthday.)

Well they're individually wrapped in their own individual white papers with no caustic lettering to spoil the latex. The nipple end is fat and it stares at you thru its powdery finish while the rest of it coils in preparation for the onslaught of flesh. The powder's a lot like unbleached flour so an experiment worth doing sometime is cooking with it if you have enough of it to go around (wowee apple pie!) and enough uses for all the bags that go with it. Flour costs the most in Afghanistan so it might be wise to take along a hefty carton of Royal Knights next time you visit Kabul.

Okay so on it goes and you're ready for some fancy penile footwork and you don't even have to be careful cause there's another one in the package if it happens to rip before penetration. A little foreplay and some fingering—and maybe some eating to get it all really, really wet—and you're ready to stick in the sausage. Hup, hup, hup and you're adrift in coozle like you never felt before: the sensitivity's great! Almost as good as if you stuck a piece of tracing paper around your gong before inserting it into the poozle. But tracing paper wouldn't exactly be perfect because you'd have to seal it somehow and that would mean staples or glue or costly tape and it might just tear anyway during particularly rough in-and-outing. But you could do some tracing of the veins inside or the hairs and it might be a real nice drawing when you unfold the paper but just the same ready-sealed bags are preferable to unsealed.

Upon removing it from the juice, Bruce, you'll notice immediately that it doesn't fall off easy but you may have trouble walking if it gets stuck to the inside of your leg. It's easier to separate it from your leg than from your third leg and make sure you have a blotter handy for all the ink that all that moisture has activated. The ink on the condom that has the name of the company on it and the disease message, the ink doesn't seem permanent. And why should it be? Yeah!

Like it might even get entirely removed inside the cunt so most likely it's gotta be non-toxic or the Pure Food and Drug Administration wouldn't have released it for use in the prevention of disease. But maybe they only deal with communicable disease and come to think of it that raises serious questions also. Like it says "Sold for the prevention of disease only" but do they mean you won't be getting it if you use it? But will *she* get it if you use it, like what if she already has it? It sure didn't prevent her from getting it and it won't prevent you if you've already got it too. So all it does is prevent you from catching it during the act so the message on the box is a stone cold LIE, and should be prosecuted in a court of law.

And not only that, it's *sexist* too! Like it oughta do something about her affliction (like there could be either medication for her clap or syph or whatever the case may be or there could at least be a prescription for it on either the rubber itself or the box it comes in: a gift prescription) and not just keep you happy in the security of knowing you'll be disease-free just cause you're a male, y'know? And it's sexist in a second dynamite way too. Say you're cheating on your honey and the only way she'll ever know is if you contract a bug or two and spread it to her cavity. You don't ever have to worry about that possibility if you keep your pork sheathed. Unless it breaks but if it breaks *it's all over anyway*. That's if you wear it when you stick your doodle in the other one so you don't catch it to begin with. Or if you catch it to begin with you can wear it while you're stickin it in your old lady during the time when you're undergoing treatment and she'll never know the difference. But if *she* ever recommends that you wear one watch out: it means she's been taking *you* for a ride!

Well there is a method—albeit illegal—whereby no disease is even remotely possible for either party (providing of course no pustules are already present in the gonad region) to contract venereal scourge. And that method is jerking off with the bag on. If you're a biblical scholar and you wanna avoid the sins of Onan this is the way since you won't have to spill the seed on the ground (in this case it's *extremely* important that there be no holes in the merchandise). In fact it's fun and it lasts a lot longer than when you sock it to her hole cause you control the friction and the strokes and so it's bound to be a good one.

Okay it's pud yanking time so get to it. You don't have to roll it down all the way cause you don't have to give a shit whether any of it leaks out. Four fast strokes to start things off and a pause and a squeeze. Followed immediately by 52 more just as fast. Then 50 slightly slower but with more gusto. And 125 all-out hard ones next to test the product's reliability under pressure. 94 more of the same and your interest's already beginning to wane, not to mention your hard. So then you give it 14 tugs left handed and real slow but it still ain't gettin you anywhere. So you go over to the bed and lie yourself down comfortably and start thinkin about that time whatsername sucked your pecker til it was dry and meanwhile head for the hills with your pulling. At the 252 mark the first indications of the coming tide get to throbbing. At 277 the first spurt of jizz. It's all over at 291.

(Has anybody ever studied the inverse relationship between writing and masturbating, or at least writing about masturbating while masturbating and masturbating? They should, it's a fertile field for study and study leads to diplomas and other honors as well.)

Take off the used non-lamb's intestine and the ink hasn't even run cause there wasn't any stuff around to make it run except your hand and if your hand was dry it was dry. But it does run a-plenty when you turn on the faucet to water test it—and, incidentally, it passes with honors—but if you're extra neat about it and keep the water on the inside—the ink's on the outside—it won't even run!

One of the reasons in the first place for wacking off in it is the fact that it gets bunched up during anti-procreative conjugal relations and some ladies of taste object to such interference with pleasure. In other words *some gals don't like the way it feels in their orifice* so it's advisable to save your Royal Knight for other purposes only. But if you do happen to slip it into a cunny by hook or by crook it's useful in more ways than one. It's so when you're finished the only stuff on your prong is your own stuff so if you collect dried cum you got the pure stuff right there at hand to dry without any alien substances to fuck with the drying time.

Also a feature with Royal Knights: no rubber odor, no smell of tires, no chewable rubber band ambience. It could just as easily be fiber glass. It smells less like rubber than an East New York Savings Bank bank book cover. Four days after use it smells like Bisquick biscuits and that's even after the flour powder stuff's been gone for days!

# Black Music/White Audience

Andy Zimmer was a veteran of two suicide attempts by the fall of '63. Once he got fed up with being fat and unwanted so he swallowed an entire bottle of aspirin and, thinking it would do the trick, went to sleep with a smile on his face. The next morning it took 10 minutes for his parents to wake him and he had a stomach ache for a week. There was nothing left to do but lose some weight, comb his hair different, hang around with the cuties and get excellent grades. But it still didn't ease the hunger in his heart and new torment was on the horizon anyway. His brother who he never liked died in a car accident 100 miles away and he tried to jump out the window because of a heap of guilt feelings. They restrained him from leaping so that doesn't count as a genuine suicide attempt but at least there was one good one. He was from Flatbush or Midwood or somewhere.

He checked in at C.W. Post and lived in the same hall of the dorms as Borneo Jimmy, then a Ray Charles madman. Andy liked Jerry Butler but preferred Garnet Mimms. He was on the soccer team and was doing real good until his appendix laid him low. Some guy with a car charged well-wishers 25¢ apiece to see him at the hospital. There were three takers and it was Halloween so they stole him some pumpkins. He showed everybody his postoperative shaven crotch. It was a novelty but he was not proud but it was all he had. Except for his 45's. The newest of which happened to be "Cry Baby" by Garnet Mimms. He played it and went for long walks alone at night in his black sneakers. Nobody wore them then. He played Garnet Mimms until one of his two roommates broke it with a machete. What has Garnet Mimms done since then? Who knows but Andy has had more hard times.

He went to the Apollo with David Roman over the Easter vacation and he said to his next seat neighbor "James Brown has soul." Two rows of black faces turned around and stared at him. He got his butt stomped. He got ripped off for 14 bucks. The 14 bucks had been in his shoe but in the scuffle it was removed. He had to bum 15¢ to get home, shoeless, on the subway. When he got home he wanted to play the Shirelles but he forgot he had left his record player at school.

By '65 he was smoking pot, flipping out on morning glory seeds and digging Joe Hinton. He caught Joe and Bobby Blue Bland at a (safe) Tuesday afternoon show at the Apollo. Two years later he went to see the Grateful Dead at the Cafe au Go Go because some joker told him that Pigpen was another Otis. Now he's married to his Coney Island Baby (where'd she come in?) and he's working as an office flunky on Wall Street. If you give him anything for Christmas why not make it a complete set of Garnet Mimms (Andy was a boxing fan back in high school and there was a middleweight back then by the name of Holly Mims but he wasn't very good), maybe he'll be able to start all over, as Tyrone Davis would say.

Oh yeah he once looked up Jocko Henderson in the Philadelphia phone book, gave him a buzz, but it turned out to be the wrong Jocko Henderson (there are more than one). Another time he called up Wand Records and asked for Chuck Jackson. Chuck wasn't there so he asked the guy when the next Chuck Jackson LP would be out. The guy said wait a minute, he had to check, he came back in 10 minutes and said I don't know.

# A Fatal Jerkoff on the Moon

There was this party for Robert Mapplethorpe at the Chelsea and there was a shopping cart full of cans of Budweiser rolling around and guys were starting to snap em open. Plus they would drink em. Well then somebody dumped an ounce of boo on the table and cats and kitties got their kicks that way and the beering halted. Well then Todd Rundgren lit a match. He stuck the match down there with the ounce and he was still holding it so's he could get a good fire going without the light going out. There weren't too many matches left. Well no sooner had the ounce fire gotten off the ground than the area was mobbed with grass fans opposed to the blaze. And it wasn't cause they were Smokey the Bear types, it was cause if there was gonna be a fire they wanted it inside a joint. Jesus the world sure has a mile of weird creatures with even weirder preferences! And they were all lined up around the forest fire even though it wasn't a forest. Some people used to call it a forest when it was just seeds and stems—mostly stems—because that's the way it looked. This wasn't even a forest, it looked a lot more like lawn mower cuttings shredded up even more. Some people like it like that but Todd saw thru their dumb game and he was having the most fun at the party. There was even a joint made up of a dollar bill with the stuff rolled up in it, if the stuff was gonna get smoked it would have to be under unusual circumstances or over Todd's dead body. And he wasn't gonna die for anybody. In fact it was a whole lot like that one where Mr. Natural tries to throw the TV set out the window and everybody stops him. He got stopped dead completely and he had to leave but not Todd. Todd prevailed and prevail he did.

But when he was a kid he used to get beat up on by this meany named Bruce. So when he grew to being older he never liked people named Bruce but he liked me anyway even though Bruce was my middle name. Which means he's sure a good guy. Did I say he was a good guy? I mean he was a good guy. He used to be a real short guy when he was a kid and usually guys who are real short grow up to be perverts so they can take it out on the world.

Not Todd. He grew up to be unshort, he just willed it and he grew some extra inches and they added up to feet. Funny because when you're producing Jesse Winchester and others of that ilk they let you sit down so it doesn't matter how tall you are. And since Todd's done that sort of thing he's been allowed the privilege of the chair more than once. But you can't sit down all the time or your legs would never unbend. And you need good legs for rock and roll or even just walking down the street.

Such as the streets of Great Neck. That's where he lived when he was with the Nazz and the main drag there is called Middle Neck Road. Most of the cheap food there is in supermarkets but for gourmets there's this place called Kuck's. Not Kucks as in the name of that guy Johnny Kucks who used to pitch for the Yankees in the World Series but Kuck's. As in Mr. Kuck. Well this guy Kuck was a Mormon by trade and he used to go to his store at around 4:30 AM in order to get the jump on his competitors. Wait a minute, he wasn't a Mormon, he was a Christian Scientist but he went to the Christian Science Convention when it was in Salt Lake City where all the Mormons live their polygamous lives or die trying. Kuck used to shove that ugly Christian Science *reading matter* in people's faces. That may be okay and well and good in the waiting room of the Poughkeepsie railroad depot but it ain't exactly fun when food's on your mind. Nothing beats food and Kuck knew that food and fun were worth bucks in his pocket. So he used to charge 59¢ for a can of potato sticks that other places charged 17¢ for and he always got it because rich dippos would pay it rather than rub up against minorities in the supermarket. On Halloween the local kids still throw eggs at Kuck but they buy the eggs elsewhere. He always follows people (meaning kids) all around the store to make sure they don't steal anything. Such as the cheese-covered almonds which are good and you should try them but don't buy them at Kuck's. They're about a dollar there. Andy Winters of the late Soft White Underbelly once bought them but it was somebody else's money so it was okay. They were the other band in town. The Nazz was the other one. Todd was in it and you know what else he used to call Kuck's? He used to call Kuck's *Kooks* as in Kookie lend me your comb. Pretty good, huh? But it didn't lessen the situation foodwise.

For instance the only hamburger meat in the place was patties, not meat. Patties are mostly soy bean crud. They cook up quick because they're so thin and the Soft White Underbelly preferred them but not the Nazz. Todd never ate them but he likes the name Patti anyway, particuarly when it's attached to the name Smith. He likes Patti Smith a whole lot and she was at the Robert Mapplethorpe party too. Robert's art stuff was good too, real good in fact and one of the things had a long bent male mutton dagger with the balls hanging over a sharp edge. Geez that must hurt! And there was some poon stuff too with paint over it sprayed on thru some sort of grid like the ones they use for spaghetti. There wasn't any spaghetti there at the Chelsea and there weren't even any pretzels, just beer. Kuck's used to be the favorite beer buying spot for late-nite drinking after the other places closed for both the Nazz and the Underbelly included.

What else about Todd? Well the only other thing about him is his music and where he lives. He lives in L.A. in Nicholas Canyon or someplace like that. Ask any stranger on the street in Hollywood where Nicholas Canyon is—or even Watts for that matter—and they won't know. Because L.A. is all spread out. And so is his house. It's spread out and he has two refrigerators full of Dos Equis at all times, just in case somebody wants to start a party. The way L.A. is spread out is kind of like the way Long Island is spread out and after all Great Neck is a member of Long Island. So you need a car to get around but Todd doesn't need one. Todd gets around just as easy with no car in his garage.

But that's not where he was born. He was born in Upper Darby, Pennsylvania. But that's not where he was born either, he lived there but he was born somewhere else but where he was born is a mystery. Nobody knows where he was born including myself. Or if they do they're not talking. Well Upper Darby is where he lived and it's near Philadelphia, home of Frankie Avalon and Smokin Joe Frazier and Fabian Forte and Dick Clark. Todd's never been invited to the *Dick Clark Show* even though he's got a city in common with the stupid goon. Something like that once happened to Bobby Vinton. Bobby's originally from Canonsburg, Pa. It's a suburb of Pittsburgh and Perry Como grew to fruition there too and Bobby's dad was once the leading bandleader in the greater Pittsburgh area. Yet Perry never let Bobby on his show despite all the million sellers and the musical excellence. Well so the Bobby Vinton Fan Club put their two cents in the next time Perry arrived at the airport. They had these signs that read "Bobby Vinton, the greatest singer in the world" and was Perry ever embarrassed! Yet today Bob and Perry are living right near each other again on—of all places—Long Island! What a small world.

Well so it's obvious Todd could get all his fans together and do the same thing next time Dick Clark lands at L.A. International and they can have signs urging Dick to take Todd back to Philly with him for the Saturday afternoon show from coast to coast. Dick's watched as much in L.A. as anywhere else and the folks in Todd's new home town would sure enjoy seeing him perform live via satellite or however they do it from East to West. But Todd isn't that way at all so don't you go ahead and do it if you're one of his fans. Todd just wouldn't wanna see dumb Dick treated so bad, he's a damn nice guy. Todd is, Dick isn't but blessed are the creeps.

And as far as the music goes there's this bird named Brownie who's either a sparrow or a finch and he lives indoors because he was found weak and unable to fly very far. He was flying into a revolving door at a Horn & Hardart and somebody almost stepped on him but a young lady picked him up and brought him home and now takes care of him. She feeds him hamburger meat in thin strips like worms and he eats it up. He likes fruit cocktail too and enjoys hearing his chirps played back on a tape recorder. And his taste in music is pretty good too. His little keeper used to leave the radio on to keep him company when she was away and it was always on a muzak station like WPAT or WRFM and then she tried WPLJ and Brownie preferred the muzak to that. But finally Brownie discovered "Wailing Wall" on Todd's *The Ballad of Todd Rundgren* album and now he'll listen to nothing else. Whenever it's on he'll stop whatever he's doing and he concentrates fully on both the words and the music and the singing and the playing. And it's followed by "The Range War" which reminds his petmistress of Carole King so she likes it a whole lot. So her and Brownie have a whole lotta fun with those two cuts and they play them incessantly whenever they get the chance. And I kinda like the cut after those two, "Chain Letter," so the three of us get along just fine.

(By the way "Wailing Wall" may seem like a yiddle song but it's not even though that's what the title seems like.)

Other than music and living he's got hobbies too, foremost of which is reupholstering sofas in original designs. "It's an awful lot of fun. Of course I get attached to some of them occasionally and twice I've kept them instead of selling them or giving them away. But they never get to know you or respond to you when you call their name or any of that." I asked him if raising fabrics from the fabric store shelf to the best couches in town had anything to do with producing luminaries like the Band which he does whenever Robbie Robertson isn't in the mood. He said no.

As a result he's one of the top five itinerant hotdoggers based in other than New York. The others are Tom Nolan, Dave Newberger, Charley Payne (hey Charley give me a ring or drop me a line care of Straight Arrow or if you know him tell him to do it) and Howie Klein. No three of them have ever been at the same place at the same time and only two of them are in the recording business, Todd and Tom. Todd's contributions are well known and documented but not Tom's. Tom did some yelling during the mastering of the Woodstock version of Sly doing "Higher" and his voice is on the album yelling "higher" along with the rest of them. Only one of the five is affiliated in any way with Albert Grossman and that's Todd. He's also the only one who was ever in the Nazz. They did this great song called "Open My Eyes" or something like that and all of Long Island was singing it for a while. Kathy Streem who's now John Wilcock's secretary was just a teen then and she used to hang around outside the Nazz homestead because she couldn't figure out how to get inside. But she's got a good figure, a very good one in fact. Maybe Todd would have given her a tumble if he had looked out the window at the right time.

Since that time three Nazz albums and two Todd albums have graced the pantry. The first Todd one is called *Runt* cause that's what he calls himself because it rhymes with Rundgren or at least the first syllable. *Gren* is a lot like Grin and they have a good album out too but he's not on it. He hasn't done a bad album yet. Will he ever? God only knows but chances are he never will. Who says? Me.

Is he in it for the money? No he's in it for love. Is he moving to England real soon? Yes.

# Hot Times from Wrestling's Golden Quarter Century (1945-1970)

Starting in 1945, many of World War II's hottest buns were coming back from the krauts and japs to America's own home shores. More than 93% of these superlative citizens had seen combat and of these more than .05% had been familiarized with this combat stuff through prior ring service, as either boxers and/or wrestlers. Among the returning pugs were Lenny "Boom Boom" Mancini, wearer of the Purple Heart, and Tommy Gomez, wounded sixteen times and more relaxed in rings as a result. The cauliflower ear brigade returned Cpl. Louis Thesz and Pvt. Morris Shapiro, known to the layman as the Mighty Atlas. But those guys were already scufflers from the prewar era—legitimacy still hung heavy in their hearts.

Meanwhile there was a whole slew of newcomers to the mat who had received their baptism of fire exclusively from the armed services, guys who were innocent enough to fake their ages from 14 to 18 in order to enlist in Roger's Rangers or whatever they were called. Arnold "Golden Boy" Skoaland was one of them and so was Donn Lewin—they were ripe for the whole new era of liberated, post-legitimate wrestling, and they didn't even mind playing the roles of mere pushovers and puppets since that's all the war taught them anyway.

Boxing was just beginning to show signs of turning into a massive trillion-dollar dud, the Louis-Conn rematch of 1946 had failed to fulfill many promises at all, and eventually even promoters lost interest in conceiving and hyping "dream" matches. Local punch clubs declined and TV—a friend in need and a friend indeed as far as wrestling was concerned—started destroying things too as fight fans stopped paying to see it live.

One of the reasons club fighting (or even prior amateur experience) never had much to do with postwar wrestling was that training wasn't so essential when victory wasn't so essential.

You could lose and still you'd at least gotten some exposure, and nobody kept records—especially not Nat Fleischer. So what set postwar grunts and groans off from Stanislaus Zbyszko, George Hackenschmidt and Frank Gotch's "real thing" of way back was that being lousy and being a loser were finally no setbacks at all. Like in boxing there were always guys like Norman Cassaberry and Tommy Tibbs who lost more than they won but they were never headliners except in tank towns and after a while they were rarely even prelim creeps. But in wrestling it didn't mean nothin if you were Buddy Rosen who never seemed to win, or Arnold Skoaland who seemed to win about once out of ten.

The good-guy-bad-guy thing probably wasn't an innovation and neither was the business of heroes. Bad guys who were heroes might've been new but who the hell knows? But tag teams just had to have gained all their steam in those postwar situations which depended on the occasional ultimate superiority of an abject bad guy over a slob of a total loser. It not only led to more guys in the ring (hence more action) but it sort of (pre)tended to equalize things (at least at odd moments) if the guy who was getting his ass beat—but was honest—could tag off and get some help from another worthless cretin. The greatest fight of the entire period was a 6-man tag team match with Donn Lewin, Ted Lewin and Johnny Barend vs. the Sheik, Wild Bull Koury and Johnny Valentine. In the first fall the Sheik and Wild Bull got Barend's head through the ropes and Koury held out his legs while the Sheik knee-dropped him across the back and Valentine knocked him silly with atomic skull crushers to the head. All this time everything was on the up and up in terms of number of guys in the ring, only Koury was actually inside the ropes and Johnny V. was always outside. So the only time when the ref was able to beef about it was when the Sheik touched ground after dumping his patella on the spine of the helpless, hapless Barend. But since that didn't cover much time at all—he was quick at getting back through the ropes—and the ref had to count 10 or something before he could disqualify anybody they never got stopped.

New York State was so far behind the times that they still had wrestling under the auspices of the N.Y. State Athletic Commission. That meant that 601-lb. Haystacks Calhoun couldn't fight against two guys like he could in most places—he had to have a tag team partner and it was usually somebody meager like the Golden Boy. Their opponents were never bonafide villains, it was usually the likes of Judo Jack Terry and Danny Ferazzo. Haystacks would put his horseshoe aside but they'd always find it and give him a couple of lumps before he finally cornered them for a *big splash*—that's what he called his variety of body press. Nobody ever got up from it, that was the only thing unique about it. Most people think he never got pinned but that's false.

Another dumb thing about New York State was no female wrestling was allowed, so Madison Square Garden and West Hempstead's Island Garden never got to see the likes of June Byers. June was never dirty. There was this time when she fought in Boston and the announcer was Sam Menacher who was one of the strongmen in *Mighty Joe Young*. Not only that but Sam was also her husband and he didn't say one disparaging thing about her.

Germans and orientals were a weird sort of problem. Most of them were bad guys, but bad guys who couldn't win too often like Karl Von Hess, Ludwig Von Kropp and Fritz Von Wallach. The Great Scott's real name was Dutch Schweigart—he ran like the plague from teutonichood. On the other hand was Tokyo Joe whose big move was the karate chop (the whole karate jargon first got popularized through TV wrestling interviews and nowhere else) and whose birth certificate registered him as Phil Silver.

The most consistent winner among classic dirty fighters was Killer Kowalski, a genuine bad-ass. He once ripped off Yukon Eric's ear and he jumped on Pepper Gomez' head in what was supposed to have been a test of Pepper's stomach. He also spilled a thermos of hot coffee on Timothy Geohagen, an MD from Dublin who later described Kowalski's claw hold as operating on the liver. He got a degree in metaphysics from some school in Ontario and he was a vegetarian. By about 1969 he had grown a beard and was beginning to get pissed off that they still hadn't allowed him to win the title, venting his spleen on lily-livered announcers like Ray Morgan and Bill Cardill. He never got his big chance, even though he was most likely the best that ever walked the earth.

Now it's over, the golden quarter-century.

# Holiday for Keglers

Bowling has always had hard times attached to it. Back in the days before the original American Revolution bowling meant meetings for the discontented so the English guys banned the sport of "nine pins." So then they went ahead and added a tenth and it became ten pins, which was legal. They could have subtracted one but they added one instead and ever since bowling has been synonymous with addition. There's more addition in bowling than in boxing and badminton put together.

In the 1960's there was this guy named Kenny Selig who fought the long hard road to the top at Green Acres Bowl. He was a marathon bowler, he once bowled 80 games in one sitting. His high game was 299 but he's had 13 or 14 strikes in a row over two games. Finally he was in a big game with two locals for 200 bucks. He whipped their ass and then they told him he'd be obliged to DIE if he insisted on them paying so he didn't insist. He didn't even bowl another game as long as he lived. There was no fun in his lifeblood anymore so he called it quits.

Also he was a homebody so he didn't feel like hitting the pro bowlers tour. He could have gone to St. Louis for the U.S. Open with its top price of 8000 dollars but he did not but instead sat home as he caught the action nostalgically over teevee. Dick Ciprich eliminated Les Schissler 247 to 212 when Les's ball kept deflecting to the right, no pin action at all. Dick moved up against Wayne Zahn but in frame one Dick only got a 9 with his first ball. Of course he converted it to a spare but Wayne just shot out ahead (tremendous psychological lift!) with a strike. Then he blew it himself with a lousy 9 and a spare. Then Dick found the pocket for a very heartening 9 himself, and a spare, then a mighty impressive strike. Wayne followed with a 9, 9s were contagious all afternoon. Things were pretty even in the third, also in the fourth.

Then Wayne played for his ball to break late and it broke too early, he would have to make an adjustment or pay the price with defeat. The qualifications for the tourney were like in golf where you gotta qualify to be in it. Dick was the only league bowler who made it. Wayne won. But he was losing by 33 pins to Mike Limongello after 4. Mike's good thing was the way he did a deep knee bend at the leverage point, a calculated risk but he stayed out of trouble. In the 7th he had a little luck on that one for a strike. Meanwhile Wayne had it hooking left without a turn signal on it so the pins didn't know what to do. Many of them remained standing. If Wayne was gonna have a chance to win in the 9th he had to strike and he hit 7. A man must pull off the musts and he did not: forget him, he's no good. The name's Wayne Zahn. The place was cold and blowy St. Louis.

Tita Semiz was Mike's opponent in the finals and Tita's business-like approach had the ball right down the second arrow as it put a 10-pin lead in his pocket. Easterners don't buckle under and both boys were from that fabled part of the nation. Full pendulum armswing and a 90° knee gave Tita *3 strikes* in a row, leading to one baseball joke after another among illiterate children of sport but not the sophisticated fan and there were many. In the fourth he muffed it, kissing a 300 game goodbye. The pressure led Mike into a foolish 4-9 split. And there was nothing he could do but remain unhappy for the rest of his livelong days. Then Tita choked his way into a 5-7 split, reducing his lead to 19 pins as the game emerged as a match once more. Two strikes and Mike only trailed by 9. As it went into the final frames it was not the prize money but the prestige of victory that led these youngsters into gutsy shots that were a whisker high. The biggest ball of Tita's career and all he got was 6. He bounced it at the line and he was faced with the difficult 1-2-4-7. Then some stupid caution in the 10th and the first U.S. Open was all Mike's! He didn't win it, the other fellow lost it. That's not much of a use for bowling.

Recreation is better.

# Katmandu and Soda

There's this person named Bozo now in Katmandu who used to be the biggest dealer of you-know-what on Long Island. He once made an enormous hash deal three feet from the Suffolk County D.A. at the Oakdale Spring Carnival, that's how bold he was and the Mystic East hasn't diminished his guff. Katmandu is for a rest but before he got there he ran booze between the Indian mainland and Ceylon. There's some kind of tax situation involved and revenuers are a pain in the aorta the world over. So he smuggled the stuff across on a ferry, back and forth lots of times a day as the time allowed. But he had to pay a *baksheesh*, local lingo for a bribe, and he never got caught.

There are taxes and dry states in the U.S. of A. too, hooch can be a running concern for a youngster with ambition. After all, what's Peter Fonda or Dennis Hopper got over Robert Mitchum of *Thunder Road*?

# Good Reading Means Good Drinking

Everybody who's ever had the papaya juice at either of the Berlin Bars (2nd Ave. and 3rd Ave. on 86th St. in N.Y.C.) knows their juice isn't worth the paper *cup* it's poured into. But if the Berlin Bar they've been frequenting happens to be the one on 3rd Avenue there's no way they could have missed the great big papaya place just across the other side of 86th Street. But maybe all the reading matter has turned them away in disgust. There's a heck of a lot of words on all the walls and surfaces and if an individual is an illiterate dummy then there's every reason for him to take off quick and never come back.

But the reading *is* good, it's a lot better than Charles Dickens or John Steinbeck. Also it's shorter, it's even shorter than short stories. It's even shorter than a lot of poems. Some of it's even shorter than many sentences. Like: "Papaya a definite aid to normal regularity." Or: "Papaya: The drink of the Angels— Christopher Columbus." (Did Chris really say that? Only his descendants know for sure.) Also: "Papaya acts as a digestive aid and will eliminate such things as ulcers of the small intestine, the stomach and the bowels. Bad cases of gastritis respond quickly." And: "Papaya is God's greatest gift to man." Und: "Nobody but nobody can make a better papaya drink; 30 years of painstaking..."

That's not even ten percent of all the words written on the inside of the place, quite a bit even for a speed reader with all A's. Plus he's got to be able to digest what he reads or else it's gonna mean nothing. And if the meaning doesn't sink in he's not gonna enjoy any of the drinking that goes with it. Thankfully the reading is *easy* reading, even a dodo can understand it. And what he understands is that the management is pretty darn arrogant about its product. Is it rightly so? Yes,

Sometimes the papaya juice tastes slightly rancid or even a bit like vomit but that's exceedingly rare. Usually it's quite a liquid.

It's even better than guava juice, which they don't have any of but it's better just the same. It's also even better than cantaloupe juice, which they also don't have etc. But it's not always better than the coconut champagne. That they have. They have it in huge immense metal things with spigots on the end. One little turn and it's in your cup, a sanitary paper one that'll be used only by you. Unless you share it with a friend.

Which is a real good idea. Sharing. What's so good about it is there's so many flavors there it wouldn't be that easy to swallow a full dose of each and every one. But if you and each of your friends buy a single drink then everybody gets a couple sips of everything. And there's a whole lot of everything. There's piña colada, that's got some pineapple flavor to it and some coconut. Cott has a bottled drink called coco-pina but it *stinks* compared to the piña colada. Also there's something called pineapple juice, but it's only *called* that. It couldn't actually be pineapple juice, because pineapple juice comes from a can, right? Well it's good whatever it is. Also there's some grape but it's not really juice, it's just grape *drink*. Which goes to show they're honest in their labeling but it's a good drink anyway. They're *all* good and it would be a shame if you were friendless. If you were friendless you wouldn't be able to drink them all at one time. Not unless you were very, very parched from the heat of the sun. Or unless you didn't mind not drinking the entire cup, but that would be wasteful with people dying of thirst in Death Valley.

Actually the coconut champagne isn't actually the world's greatest quencher. It'll kill a thirst at the top of the glass but once you get down near the bottom all those coconut shreds will act like nuggets of sand. So you may have to follow it up with a papaya just to be safe. But you can *eat* the coconut residue with your finger, just don't try to drink it.

And it's not even the only eating in the place. No because they have the best dogs on 86th Street. And that's saying an awful lot because 86th Street is just teeming with German stuff and German is synonymous with dogs. Frankfurter means it's from Frankfurt, back in Deutschland über alles, so these dogs are better than the best. And the place's sign painter is kept busy announcing just that: "100% pure beef frankfurters, better than filet mignon." And they are better than steak any day of the week. And that includes Monday. They're better than Nathan's dogs (including the Oceanside Nathan's) and they're better than the dogs on Rockaway Beach Blvd. in Rockaway. The color is more authentically doglike and so's the taste and texture and juiciness. The rolls are excellent too. And the mustard! It's hot and it's not spicy but it's ROBUST. Put them all together they spell food.

And food can often build up a thirst so you'll want plenty more to drink before you're finished. And it's good to keep in mind how healthy the whole thing is: "Our Health Giving Famous drinks from Coast to Coast are made Exclusively from these Triple A Tropical Fruits, no artificials ... no synthetics." Does triple A mean it's *baseball*, Triple-A in the minors? No it means the stuff's guaranteed to be tough in superior quality, so tough it can kill mean old Mr. Sickness with one hand behind its back. But it wouldn't be easy to tie that hand back there because it's tough.

And besides that, papayas don't have arms. They're shaped somewhat like pears. How do I know? Well they have them all lined up on top of the papaya drink machine. Lined up in a circle like little children waiting for a game of volleyball. They're for sale, the papayas that is, not the children. (Hmmm ... I wonder how kids would taste ... ) And as an incentive to sales the papayas are natural and organic! Yes and not only that but the place is kept immaculately clean. There are places elsewhere which boast a full line of health foods in the natural and organic department but which are *filthy*. Mother Nature & Sons (Jerry Rubin the writer shops there) is the filthiest looking place in North America, it even features roaches crawling up and down the walls and also across sideways. They have a drink up front called "apple-papaya" but it's heavy on the apple and it's as rancid as rancid can be. If you look in the store window after hours you can make out the fact that the drink is still brewing even though it's not being drunk or sold. Which means it's gonna be *stale* by the time the place opens in the morning. The hideously dirty place (roaches carry disease). If the papaya place has roaches they're kept well hid but chances are they're kept well dead instead.

Another good thing about the papaya place is the possibilities for double parking as well as the opportunities. You can double park and nobody's gonna bother you. Except maybe all the cabs who park there too, they might block you off if you ever want to get out. Cabs are a menace and they should be removed from the city streets and roads. But cabbies gotta drink too, just like everyone else. In fact roaches gotta eat, so let's really give them an even chance too. Let's all get to know one another real well over a friendly glass of nature's own revitalizer.

# Grady Hatton's Niece Set the World on Fire

Patti Gober was Grady Hatton's niece and still is even though he isn't still much. For some reason he ended up as manager of the Houston Astros. To most residents of the sports community it was no big deal about Grady being around and to Patti it wasn't much more than that except he was her Uncle Grady and blood is much thicker than playing favorites. Besides her relationship to the dude was her relationship to one Rick the drummer of Brethren. She didn't think much of Alvin Lee but she did think much of Rick Lee who was no relation to Al. The former Rick kept his practice drum set up in her classy Chelsea apartment, they just had heads so the sound wouldn't be so loud neighbors would complain. He had to keep his hands and feet in shape even if not his sound. She once went out with Steve Paul and he said "Your mother'll hate me if I do anything with you, good night." By the time Brethren played Madison Square Garden with Buddy Miles on November 13 (a Friday) Ricky had moved out of the apartment but the fake drum set was still there and he was supposed to be dumb in the talking department, limiting his rap to a very few dumb words. Patti and Bobby Abrams were heading backstage at the concert when they ran into some 12-year-old groupies aiming for Rick so she decided not to bother going back there but later she realized that he'd be real mad if he found out she went there but didn't stop in to see him.

Which is all directly parallel to the reason the Knicks had such difficulties in 70-71 keeping up with 69-70: first time around every team just rolled over and played dead, second time around they decided to imitate the Knicks since if the Knicks can do it then anybody can do it. Nobody in the world knew it better than Baltimore (Bullets, not the town, which is a town where Patti's been on the way south to Florida on a trip that included hassles with local gun-toters along the way), as they trounced the New Yorkers by narrow margins their first two outings. Wes Unseld was never better and he did this real great thing on Cazzie Russell which led to injury to an opponent due to smart move. It was Cazzie backing into the basket right under the hoop and expecting Unseld to block him on the way up or the way down (either). Instead it was neither (Wes was brilliant enough to stay away and let a good thing happen) and Caz came down flat on the wood and he lay there in excruciating agony as officials failed to whistle it to a halt and allow the doc to have a look-see. If that had happened it would've meant no 2 points that the Bullets got downcourt but it WOULD NOT have meant any difference as far as painful injury was concerned: Cazzie was hurt so bad he thought it was his *right* wrist that was busted when it was really his left.

Consequently Patti—bored with N'Yawk—decided on the Rangers Fan Club as the most exciting way to travel.

And—by the way—she prefers to be called Patt and dig this. That's Pat (point after touchdown) plus T (touchdown for 6 points) which makes her a full 7-pointer and a sportsgal thru and thru!

# TV's Tussle for Life

When he's not busy tending to his retirement from pugilism at Rocky's Pizza Ring he's busy trying to hustle himself a TV show. The aforementioned Rocky Graziano. In his quest our paths once crossed. His and mine. He was once in a show about detectives starring Lee Bowman and he's done some nifty yogurt commercials and Brioschi too but that doesn't compare with having your own show and so he got me to think up some wonderful stupendous shows for him and the ones I came up with were many:

1. All commericals for the whole time of the show. That way it would be easy to get sponsors and there'd be a lot of moolah left over cause there'd be no show. Except the commercials.

2. Rocky goes to college.

3. Rocky has trouble getting a job, there aren't that many jobs around so he becomes a stewardess in drag.

4. Rocky as a divorce lawyer detective who gets to check out lots of hanky panky in these days of permissiveness on the screen and off.

5. A time-travel western.

6. Rocky as a rock and roll star with the pun on *rock*. Or an equipment manager.

7. Rocky as a junkie, every week it's how's he gonna get his money and where's he gonna score it.

8. Rocky as a junkie priest.

9. Computer programmer and he does the ads too and it's sponsored by computers.

10. Rocky as a barber who has to close up shop and go into another line of business because nobody gets haircuts anymore including him. New jobs (he tries a new one every week): animal trainer's assistant, cook, chiropractor practice dummy, belt salesman on 8th Street, panhandler who tells hippies his plight, guy who makes wigs for soldiers (and he always wants to give barbering another try), weight guesser at an amusement park, usher, railroad conductor, etc. And he always gets fired.

11. Rock as a champion chess player who can't figure out how he does it.

12. Bud Abbott!: Bud Abbott & Rocky Graziano (Bud Abbott's not dead yet).

13. A hypochondriac who gets a different fake disease every week.

14. An eccentric millionaire who collects weird things, gives away money to revolutionary causes, goes places.

15. Music teacher.

16. Auto mechanic who thinks about crimes as he's fixing cars.

17. Prisoner in a jail, maybe even on The Rock. He tries escapes, meets old friends, one week a female arrives by accident.

18. Rocky as a fashion model.

19. Double role where he plays both a marriage counselor and a divorce court judge.

20. Fireman.

21. Opera star who's awful and whose popularity is inexplicable to fellow musicians.

22. Comic book collector who fantasizes out of the stories. Including love comix.

23. Quiz show with 3 contestants, each one isolated, they all get a chance to answer but there's only one winner and it's whoever Rocky decides to like cause he can't keep track of who answered what or any of that. Usually it's the glamor doll who takes the prize. And the losers get *nothing* so the going can get really sadistic.

24. Door to door salesman.

25. Garbage man with Ralph Meeker as his sidekick. He looks thru famous people's garbage and saves stuff he likes and one week he runs into special guest A.J. Weberman.

26. Zoo-keeper or a pet show starring either a gorilla or a snake who saves the day.

27. Guy on welfare.

28. Lives with an unwed mother, has to hide the shoes every time the welfare case worker guy comes.

29. Contest winner, everything happens to him thru entering contests, clipping coupons, free samples, writing jingles, 25 words or less.

30. Mailman (who reads people's mail), Ray Heatherton as a guest and also Joey Heatherton.

31. Rocky as a burglar, thief, kleptomaniac, shoplifter.

Well so me and the Rock proposed all 31 to this cat by the name of Eddie White who produced a Broadway spine tingler by the name of *Fever Tree* or *Summer Tree* or something about a tree or the summer. He wouldn't let Rocky near his daughter. Rocky's always scratching his belly and his hair is unruly and his shirt is unbuttoned and he wears funny hats and he still talks about that date he once had with Audrey Meadows so he asked Eddie if Eddie could get him Audrey for the show. Nope and dig this: Eddie had no intention of doing anything with Rocky except one particularly no good piece of shit show that was gonna star him and Martha Raye. Martha Raye!

Rocky didn't even want Martha Raye and he didn't want Ann Sothern either cause she was known to be obese. Okay so here's what Eddie had in mind for the name of this great show about Rocky and Martha running the pizza place: *Goombah*!!! I mean! Well so they wanted me to go scouting around Rocky's pizza place and check out what else they could do to spice up the show and while we're on the subject of spices everybody knows the phrase "Variety is the spice of life." But that ain't much of a statement cause there's a lotta spices so it's just like saying "Variety is the variety of life," it would be more of a statement if it was "Variety is the oregano of life" or "Porcelain is the spice of life" or something.

So I went and checked out the Rock's pizza palace and it's the best in the city of N.Y. It's one of only a handful of pizza places that aren't also Italian restaurants that have bathrooms for pissing and shitting in even though the men's room was out of order on that occasion. The pizzas are by the round, round 1 is cheese and round 6 is pepperoni but there's nothing but space between round 8 (onions) and round 15 (special). There could easily be squid and scungilli in there somewhere and also an olive oil pizza and an olive pizza.

Okay so I come back from there and my proposal is that there be a black female pizza assistant in the place to assist him and Martha if not to *replace* Martha altogether. Eddie sez nope to that and Rocky sez it's okay with him but it would lose him his fans of the same extraction as himself. Where do you go from there? You don't, you abandon TV forever.

Oh yeah, left one out. Number 32 is Rocky as a bartender.

# The Wonderful World of Booze

Liquor by the drink has been voted into law, but until all approved liquor licenses have been granted, the following holds true in many cases.

Many hotels, restaurants and motels operate private clubs where the sale of mixed drinks is allowed, and provide membership cards to guests when introduced or accompanied by a member. Guest membership requirements vary, but the cost is usually nominal. In public restaurants, you can bring your own liquor, available in package stores, and the management will provide the necessary set-ups. You must bring your own vermouth, however. Drinking in all public places is not permitted after 2:15 a.m. Liquor stores are open every day but Sunday. Restaurants affiliated with clubs where liquor by the drink is served are designated by a replica of an empty cartridge pen.

And when you buy, buy rye. Cause once again it's that time of the year for rye, be it winter, summer, spring, fall or monsoon season. It's the one drink that'll whittle away a hot day in the sun or make a rainy, snowy, misty day go faster—or slower depending on you. Three quarters of a quart may not be enough for one day's ordinary consumption once you get going. And there's no better place to have it than in Rye, New York, just 15 minutes over the Throggs Neck Bridge. There may or may not be a highway toll before you get there but most likely it's just the 25¢ required for the bridge. Rye crackers would go a long way towards making it the dream vacation you've always wanted, even if only for an hour or two. But things might get so pleasant you'll decide to rearrange your entire life and rye will be what did it. Give it a try.

And here's the story. The Flying Burrito boys sure as all heck took the big roots plunge when they headed out past psychedelia to country, a Root that's as famous as you can get. Yet they hesitated along the way and never did make it all the way to crew cuts (and/or greaserhood) and the Grand Ole Opry. Same thing goes for the liquid refreshment Root. In fact most young dopers haven't yet gotten much beyond Ripple and Bali Hai, which is a shame and a pity cause there's a whole universe there, with such show stoppers as gin, zubrovka, sloe gin fizz and Underberg bitters.

Yet there are oldtime favorites which would undoubtedly make any roots chart that are as lame as a sick dog. One such beverage is ouzo. It's Greek and it's famous and it's old as the hills, if not as old as time itself. The fame of ouzo depends on the fact that it's foreign, it's Greek and Greece is where *Never on Sunday* took place. There can't be any other reason for its rep, since ouzo is certainly no Jim Dandy of a great drink. Maybe it once was. If it was then now it's a hasbeen. Here's what it'll do for you: put you to sleep. You know what else does that? A punch in the head. So you can avoid it, it's nothing but hype. A better choice would be Bacardi rum, Marty Balin's favorite drink.

*Alcohol and gasoline don't mix* unless you're driving to or from a bar or liquor store, in which case they mix even better than butter and sand. The further you drive the better the booze feels when you get there and the better prepared you are for the long ride home. Why should it be any other way? And why shouldn't your car companion be Bacardi's? Since you're on the move it can't be a mixed drink which is all the better. Water, fruit juice and soda pop are just camouflage. In fact it's extra liquid bulk, never to be desired unless you're planning on making more piss stops than necessary. Straight from the bottle you can confront all 80 of its proof in all its smoking intensity. All you'll need is 13 to 15 shots and welcome aboard, you've passed over the gap to alcoholic oblivion which is one of the best oblivions the distillers have to offer.

You take your first shot of Bacardi's. Maybe it doesn't do a goddam thing to you just yet. Maybe, on the other hand, it *does*. And it can in any number of ways. For example, it might cause you to cough during, before, or after you belt it down. Or gulp. Maybe it's even the very first shot of anything you've ever had the enormous pleasure of putting away in all your natural born days and it seems like real genuine *pain*. It is. But what's a little pain when you're en route to blowing your mind, Jack? You'll even, with a little experience, learn to live with it or even get beyond it, it won't hurt no more. That's a goal to shoot for. But you might be one of those lucky Joes who stand up for a ride on their surfboard the very first wave. In that case it'll go down real smooth, or almost real smooth. You might be getting deceived by the ease, or maybe not. Maybe you're one of those gifted personalities to whom booze will always be easy as pie. Congratulations if this is the case. But if it's not so easy take it slow, it will improve as you spend some time with your drinking. If not, then just focus on the *effect* you're after, make believe it isn't poison (food is poisoned too, so don't worry about life and death any more than you're accustomed to) or just belt a lot down real quick so you get numbed into forgetting about it. Or, here's an excellent suggestion for the booze novice, get stoned beforehand in a more conventonal way and maybe that'll give you a helping hand.

One item not all boozerias have ready on hand is the number one easy-down shot-after-shot liquid heat: Pernod. Whether you spell it with a capital P or small it spells instant pleasure in any language, not just the tongue of France where it comes from. It's the drink of a thousand faces, which you might expect since it's the little brother of absinthe, now outlawed even in La Belle Paree. Absinthe has been known to wear away a marble table top so you know it's gotta be something special. So's pernod even though it's soothing to the tongue and palate. Yet it's tricky so be prepared. First hit might be an unpleasant one, either flavorwise (heavy on the licorice) or heatwise (it's a whopping one hundred proof). It's never the same twice in a row so next time it's tasteless, odorless and soft as water. Soon enough you'll be building up a high that you may very well recognize as *psychedelic*! Yes that's right and it's 100% legal and it's bright yellow in color, very bright in fact. Mix it with water and a few cubes and it's milky, murky light yellow, a living mystery in fluid form.

Pernod'll mix well with anything and by mix I don't mean in the same glass at the same time but rather the one at a time sequence known as mixing your drinks. The oldtimers frown upon it, say it leads to adventures in puke, don't pay them no mind, they're fools of the worst sort. Pernod will mix with all of the following: bourbon, vodka, whisky, applejack, vermouth, cognac, anisette, crème de menthe, Châteauneuf-du-Pape, gin, rum (even Hudson Bay Rum, 151 proof), chianti, pineapple brandy, scotch, minted gin, Galliano, banana liqueur, beer. Beer, while not an aficionado's notion of the real live booze, contains more than enough alcohol for most purposes, including getting bombed out of your skull, you just have to slurp down more of it than with the other stuff and have a bottle or other receptacle handy for passing water once the emergency arises. Your bladder deserves a break so be good to it.

As far as beers go in terms of *this* beer or *that* beer you can drink day and night, night and day, you can search the wide world over and still not find the perfect beer. The reason for that is simple: beer is just an approximation . . . like a good cigar it can only hint at the *possibly better*, find that one and it'll point you towards the *possibly best* but do you know what? There's no such thing! If there were you wouldn't be drinking Rheingold at the drag races, you'd be sneaking in bottle after bottle of Porter Champlain, direct from Quebec, Canada, and it wouldn't be any better and just consider the extra expense. One's as good as another for all practical purposes. One of the purposes is drinking while drunk. In which case they're all the same. But for drinking *before* drunk that's an altogether different matter, in which case *any beer from the keg* (even the worst) is leaps and bounds ahead of *any beer in a bottle or can* (even the best). We all know, however, that preferences are part of the illusory world of illusion, they have no basis in reality so you can throw all the betters and bests right out the window and drink whatever you want cause it's all good! That includes Olympia, Coors, Busch Bavarian, Pabst, Kirin, Tudor, Old Vienna, Kronenbourg, Dia-Beer, Eastside, Hamm's, Sullivan, Cardiff, Duke, Ballantine (not half bad on tap), and Whitbread.

Next up the ladder of alcoholic content is wine, fine or otherwise. Judging simply from the bottles of used grape lying around the sidewalks of the world, Gallo Swiss-Up has got to be about the best. Any must-drink list not including this pearl of a great toke ought to be scrapped and thrown in the ocean. There are no oceans in Switzerland and in fact there is no Swiss-Up there either, unless some enterprising young import-export rogue is hip to what's good. There are white grapes and there are green grapes but there are fewer than 4 white grape wines in the entire globe. That doesn't mean there are few white wines, that would be a lie. It does mean that white wines from green grapes are not only possible but abundant, those booze scientists sure must know their business. After all they've come up with Swiss-Up and in so doing solved a crucial problem: how do you stop fermenting? This is not always crucial, after all those foreigners in the wine trade don't give a hang about consistency, their wines can be different depending on such irrelevant stuff as age and patience in not uncorking your bottle until the time is right. Who has a lifetime to wait, time is now! Therefore Gallo has what it takes, no cork (you don't need a cumbersome corkscrew in your pocket wherever you travel) and no waiting. How do they do it? The secret is they've harnessed the dread chemical arsenic and made it peaceful just like the atom, they use it to stop that lousy yeast from fermenting its arse off, thus guaranteeing you each and every bottle of Swiss-Up being *exactly* the same. At least there's one thing in this crumbling universe you can depend on.

Should you drink it from the bottle or the glass? Often a dilemma, but decided for you in one direction when you're far away from home and all the paper cup stores are closed for a holiday. If the neck is narrow drinking turns into sipping and sipping is for *punks*. Glug glug glug is better than sipping but there's even a further step upwards en route to down the throat with the greatest of ease. Seek the right angle at which you can pour it down the gullet as if it were from a glass. Sometimes an angle of anything more than 0 degrees will do, depending on how fast you want it out the nozzle, even less than 0 degrees measured against the horizontal can do the trick too, but 20-30 + is pretty close as far as that goes. 60 degrees is a great angle too, 90 isn't. Experiment for yourself, it's not a closed book.

Experimental ordering of drinks is a guaranteed success too, that's if you're trapped in a restaurant somewhere and need an escape without leaving your seat. Check out the drink list and remember that anything with a good name can't be bad. Say you order a Rob Roy. You've ordered yourself a mighty fine quencher, you might've figured it for a green and red plaid treat but Mother George if it isn't something just as good: scotch and vermouth, some folks know it as a Scotch Manhattan. Two good names, two good drinks, actually it's one great drink which has two great names, either way you can't go wrong. Pink Lady, Singapore Sling: two more good ones and you *can* judge a mixed hooch by the name up front, when you've got booze mixed in with creativity—the T.A. Edisons and A.O. Stanleys of the booze world dreaming up awesome concoctions with dynamite monikers to boot—the honesty comes in plethora only! One piece of advice: pass up martinis at Howard Johnson's, they go with trouble like an uncle with an aunt.

If your uncle was the one and only Andrew Jackson then your family has a heritage of knowing its bourbon. And that bourbon is Old Crow, now available for everyone regardless of social status. Its taste will at first be vaguely familiar, reminiscent of Halo shampoo. Therefore it's tailor-made for today's longhair, a now drink for those with the strength to be contemporary in their tastes. Perfect for parties and informal gatherings, it's a necessary item for all commune basement bars. Not just for the mouth and stomach, it's a great tonic for the head as well. Old Crow and the devil (the very same devil found in each and every one of us) have a lot in common: loss of self-control, difficulty in handling furniture, sex and barbarism, violent disruptive acts, happiness and fun, far fuckin far fuckin out imagination, chills and tremors, belief in the supernatural, the body as pumice, deep sleep, anger at those who do you dirt, brotherhood and friendship, singing and dancing, talking comes easy, loss of memory, nearness to death, closeness to the floor, desire to spend money like it was chewing gum, etc. Regular use of the stuff may therefore be just what the doctor ordered in the way of helping you locate your own horns and tail and showing you what to do with them.

The main thing you can go and do is *act*, no wasting your time on 15-20 seconds of worthless relevant thought, just immediate action. What could be more vital to the revolution than the potential for immediate action, particularly when brought about by legally sanctioned means to make things even easier? Just imagine 5, 10, 20, 30 thousand students, each one of them soused on moonshine and swinging a bottle in a very wide circular motion, scaring the butts off administrators. Broken glass, pools of barf, slipping and sliding, corks being thrown in all directions, a good deal of blood and sickness, good spirit everywhere. They're not gonna take no for an answer. Say they invite the board of trustees to their little party, offer them gin and tonic or a vodka and tangerine. Can they refuse? Would they refuse? Of course not, it's their favorite means of a good time and they know what's good. After hoisting a couple of cool ones they'll be on their way towards a concession or two, maybe more. And you can't fool a drunk so it's no nonsense across the board. Try to fool a guy who is stewed *and* has right on his side and you're in for a fight man. And a bottle in hand is a distinct advantage whether full or empty. Athletes can get kicked off the football team for as much as a swig of brew passing their lips but just plain students can get away with anything while the hapless, helpless campus authorities just sit or stand there on the receiving end. All they'll be able to do is reach into their drawer for a nip from their private stash and then they'll be more vulnerable than ever.

And when you wanna *loosen up* rather than introspect or perceive like a sonofagun, booze has it over dope going away. Not just the way the Beach Boys have it over Tommy James but the way God has it over an apartment house. Say you've got a heavy date coming up, or a deadline to meet, or some homework to do, or an important interview to conduct with a great big star. You can light up some bush, you can gobble a down, you can breath deeply, *or* you can imbibe off a nearby nozzle. The last is what's preferable, it'll prepare you for the big showdown by blowing your blues away, far away, and getting the right juices flowing in the right direction. Juices have a lot to do with it since the organ of drink is the liver, and who knows more about juice flow than Dr. Liver?

The one thing booze won't do for you is the fabulous rush, there's no such thing as a booze rush. Regrettable but true. Truth is unavoidable and inescapable so for just that purpose snuff is around and ready to be used. Snuff is everything tobacco could be but isn't in cigarette, cigar and pipe tobacco form. Chewing tobacco is somewhere in between, it gets you off, it gets you high but it takes a number of seconds to do the trick. With snuff it's immediate, a vast advantage over sitting around drink after drink and eventually discovering you're drunk. The disadvantage involved in chewing tobacco is for the uninitiated it means nearly instant hangover in addition to nearly instant gratification, including the wonderful world of puke/vomit. Snorting's much better and snuff comes in many flavors. Many? It comes in *hundreds* but the American varieties (Garrett, Copenhagen, etc.) are not only unrated but unratable on an international snuff scale: they merely suck rat's ass. Good stuff comes under the name

Smith, a familiar name and finally it denotes something good other than Patti, and Fribourg & Treyer is even better (their Étrenne is synonymous with guaranteed rush—once you've stopped sneezing and started snorting from scratch—plus a good chance at a 2-hour subsequent buzz).

Yet there is a drink that supplies, right out of a bottle, the next best thing to the great rush in the sky, that's a continuous series of moment to moment flashes. The drink is tequila, the effect is you're lying on your back constantly spinning in both directions if not all 7, at the same time all the time. It's when you try to switch direction that the spatial flashes hit, and you can't catch up with yourself even if you're the great Paavo Nurmi. You're always at least a step ahead of yourselves and it's a track meet from start to finish, very much like the much vaunted lysergic. And it's a real cultural leveler, you don't have to be a hippie to love it. Tequila and tonic is rapidly becoming the favorite aperitif among camera crews in Hollywood. William H. Toast is given credit by most Hollywood historians for having started this drinking habit on so wide a scale. Not Schweppes, but Quintonic, is what he himself chooses as his mixer. His favorite tequila? Gavilan of course. From his comfortable *chaise longue* Mr. Toast suggests that you "remove the tradition of the lemon (and salt) from tequila boozing and you've made it an American drink. The Mexicans may have been there first, but we people north of the border have taken the longest strides in recent years. I don't think they're out of the running, though, but I tell you one thing. It's not likely. But if they should pull off a breakthrough in the old cactus juice, all the more power to them." Gee you can't help tripping over Old Man Humor when the subject is John Barleycorn and his friends.

Hey they don't allow it in prisons, do they?

# 2700 Music Lovers Are Dumb Bunnies

While Simon & Garfunkel may be hell and gone as far as musical relevance is concerned, each one is individually making the rounds right now as the butt of a true-life joke. Paulie Simon, according to the one that makes a mockery of him, was once invited to dinner by the one the only Al Kooper, whose wife according to rumor has become quite a fan of french ticklers. Al's parents were both along for the ride too and Al's pop is apparently somewhat of a wiseacre. Conversation inevitably moved to how "Mrs. Robinson" had gotten Paul a chance to throw out the first ball at Yankee Stadium one year because of the line about Joe Dimaggio, once the lord and master of Miss Marilyn Monroe. Well Pa Kooper wasn't one to let that go by, no sir. "Oh, so *that's* why they lowered the pitcher's mound!" (P.S. is short, y'know?) Or did they *raise* it?

Well that one's not so funny but listen to the Garfunkel one. The way I heard it is some guy from Stony Brook was driving a cab once upon a time and he had the good fortune of picking up Mr. Arthur Garfunkel. Stony Brook means hair and dope and this cabbie had it written across his face. So Garfunkel figured he could pull a little reverence out of this jivebo before the ride was thru. So he sez to the cabbie "Hey are you into music?" Well this cabbie was nobody's fool and the fact is he recognized a real rube when he saw one. Sure the cat was into music, far enough to know swill when he saw or heard it. So he went to town with Artie. "Music? Naw, I think it's all pretty lame." Artie was astounded but he retorted with a quick "*All* music? Don't you like anything?" Well that was just the opening Mr. Driver needed. "Well I'm sort of partial to acoustic duos." Ha ha and Artie's breath quickened. "Oh yeah, which ones?" Well here's the actual list the wily hackman went thru: "I like Seals & Crofts, Pacheco & Alexander, Beaver & Krause, Fraser & Debolt, Brewer & Shipley, um, let's see, Baldwin & Leps, Delaney & Bonnie but they're not exactly acoustic, Conway Twitty & Loretta Lynn, Peaches & Herb, David & Susan, Booker T & Priscilla, James Taylor & Carole King but that's only once in a while, Zager & Evans, John & Yoko, well Richard Fariña is dead but I still kinda like Richard & Mini Farinã and now there's Mimi Fariña & Tom Jans, oh yeah Marvin & Tammi too … " Well by this time Garfunkel was getting sick so he rudely interrupted the guy and told him to stop the cab, he wanted out. And he didn't even tip him!

# Luckies vs. Camels: Who Will Win?

It's easy with a pack of Camels, it's easy to tell which side is the front and which is the back. The front is the side with the camel's back on it—commonly called the hump and he's got only one, hence he's a dromedary—and the camel's left side and the camel's left side of his face and portions of all four legs and his tail. And three trees and two pyramids. And the back is the side with the buildings in town where people live (they don't live in pyramids, only dead pharaohs live there if you can call it a life).

But on the pack of Lucky Strikes both sides are identical. They both say "It's toasted" plus the Lucky Strike in a circle. Actually it's inside of four concentric circles and maybe more but there still is one way to tell which is the front. The front is the side that's facing you when the thing on top with the Indian and the letter A and "20 cigarettes" all in blue is facing you too. When the left side of the Indian's head is facing your direction and his nose is above his mouth. Otherwise it's upside down and it's the back of the pack, not the front.

Both packs have the surgeon general's warning about health on the same side and both of them have only one word beginning with a lower case piece of type and that's the word *to*. The rule is: "The only words in a title supposed to be small are articles, prepositons and conjunctions." Well to is a preposition—even Lenny Bruce knows that—and you know what? The word *that* (capitalized on the packs) is—as used—a conjunction rather than a relative pronoun so they're doing it all wrong and it's even worse than Winston tastes good like a cigarette should. Worse cause it's got the support of the prestigious surgeon general's office behind it.

But all that's quickly forgotten when it comes time for the showdown. People have always been saying that the difference between a good cigarette and a great cigarette is in the know-how. Well they may know how but you've gotta know how too. And you've gotta know how to. To light the cigarette right. And the right way is the same way as for a cigar. First if it was a cigar you'd remove the cigar band by ripping it while it's still on the cigar instead of slipping it off with a pull and a tug so you don't tear the tobacco leaf. Well a seegar is not a cigareet and vice versa so you don't have to worry about no bands, just the lighting part. And in the lighting part you take the cig (whether it's an ar or an arette) and hold it twixt the fingers horizontal with a tangent drawn to the surface of the earth below your feet. In the other hand is the match which has been lit for proper use. Hold the flame so that it's below the end of the cig you want lit but hold it low and slowly approach the cig. Don't ever let the actual flame come in contact with the cig or something bad's gonna happen to the taste of the smoke. It'll taste chemical cause chemicals are what goes into the making of the match. Just let the *heat of the match* light the cig, not the flame itself. One or more attempts may be necessary before you get it down pat but you'll notice the difference already and that's what know-how is.

Now the most important part of the smoke is when it's leaving your respiratory system out through the nose. It's crucial cause exit is the last part of the smoke you'll remember if your memory is good and if it isn't good you shouldn't be smoking. It's that tingle of warmth on the inner surface of the nostrils that does it. Like when it's in your lungs and in your mouth it's just another something in your lungs or mouth. You don't really experience the heat, same goes for the throat too. But you feel the heat to optimum watchamacallit *only in the nose* along the linings. And if heat isn't important there's no reason to set the Lucky or Camel as the case may be on fire at all, you could just as easily keep it in the ice box with the cold ham.

And the facts are that in the battle of the nose Camels are stronger to the nose, Luckies are weaker. But while Camels may be stronger, Luckies happen to be weaker. One's less weak and the other's less strong and one's more strong and the other's more weak and both are either Camels or Luckies.

Next in priorities is which is packed firmer. Luckies.

Next is which one holds moisture on the mouth end of the paper better and longer. This is important as a matter of comfort, lip comfort to be exact. Lips count too and you're not enjoying smoking pleasure if it isn't comfortable for the lip. Also worth considering in this behalf is where the moisture comes from, it comes from the tongue. It comes from the salivary glands but it's by way of the tongue. So what happens indirectly is that if a cigarette paper requires a lot of moisture to stay wet then the tongue will be getting dry in the process of keeping the lip satisfied. So while it's said that a good tobacco blend is one that won't raw the tongue (this is debatable to say the least and what's wrong with *raw*?) the fact of the matter is it's the paper too that plays a role.

The winner in the holds water longest and bestest is Camels.

Next on the agenda is will the smoke be okay if you light the wrong end and which end is wrong? The wrong end is the end with the writing on it. It's not wrong because it's not *supposed* to be lit on that end, it's wrong on account of the inconvenience caused the smoker. Cause the lettering end is the end nearest the open end of the pack and so you just plant your teeth on it and pull it out. If you had to take the time to take it out with your mitts it would be too long. So it's the wrong end. It's also the wrong end because soon after it's lit the lettering will disappear from oxidation and you won't be able to tell what brand it is.

Both brands smoke okay when you light the wrong end.

Okay next consideration is can you light them from the middle in an emergency? Yes, both will light from the middle in an emergency, in a non-emergency too. But the main emergency may be if it isn't an emergency to begin with so you get uncautious and burn your nose in so doing. The Lucky lights faster in the middle than the Camel.

Which burns faster? Well if you light both of them at exactly 4:58:05 and you lay them down unimpeded and come back at 5:07:21 you'll notice something remarkable as a tender suspender. On the one hand there's more ash on the Camel and on the other there's also more unburned portion on the Camel too! In other words they started at the same length but something extraordinary has transpired in the interim. The logical explanation is there however, it's a very good one. It's that the Lucky burns faster and it also pulls its ash with it as it burns along! So it's a most friendly cigarette, it's one that refuses to reject even its dismembered grotesque burnt end and so it wins that part of the race although that part of the race was unscheduled. Plus it already won the burns fastest part so it has two big points.

Now which has a better draw? A tie.

(A subsidiary competition with no bearing in the final decision: which is better for lighting the other without a match? To be entirely within the confines of truth it must be said that Luckies light Camels better than Camels light Luckies but you could easily turn it around cause it's not always better to give than receive. Hence inconclusive.)

Easiest on the eyes. Neither.

Pleasantest for inhaling. If mellowness is the criterion then it's Camels. If the firewood feeling is the criterion then it's Luckies. If you take out the tobacco from both and roll your own then it's as close to mellow firewood as you can get and no fire extinguisher is needed. It's a tossup here.

Now it might be stressed that tobacco manufacturers and cigarettes in particular have never (never) done anything for the armless smoker. He or she has to keep it in there tight or it falls out and gets dirty so he or she has to start a new one so as not to infect the mouth with germs. So the cig gets smoked way down to a tiny butt because the person cannot even see how far down the smoke has gone without a mirror. Thus it's important that the butt be good. Camel butts are better butts, no problem there.

CONGRATULATIONS LUCKIES FOR WINNING!

# Big Shit About Nijinsky

Like who the fuck cares about ballet except ballet fans? Nobody, not a soul, not a fuckin goddam soul. And the reason they don't is a good reason and it should be posted on all bulletin boards where entertainment is shown (including schools and showrooms) in both the city and the country. The reason is that you can forget about that hand stuff they do, it's good all right, it's even as good as the hula dancers but that's only hands and most of it's done with feet. All the feet have on their mind is where are they gonna land when they land. What goes up must come down and they have to land somewhere and they always know where. Which is exactly what happens in gym gymnastics and there's nothing as shoddy as that in all of competitive sport. Parallel bar is bad and vaulting horse is bad but floor activities are worse and all ballet is is the floor stuff with costumes on.

Just imagine if they put a tu-tu on Harmon Killebrew or a Wyatt Earp uniform on Rod Laver, that's your measure of how silly ballet is. They don't do that and for good reason. Because it is silly and they're no silly Willies even off the field. Off the field they wear normal off-the-field clothes even if they are unconventional dressers and even when they play golf. They're not gonna wear ballet slippers so why should ballet dancers wear ballet slippers?

Also there's no action and this in an action world. Particularly on stage and that includes the Living Theater, they're active even though there's no reason for it at all. Lack of reason notwithstanding, ballet oughta have the sense not to have so little action. The only action is when the guys do it real fast for the last 10-15 seconds of every ballet. They don't get dizzy but neither do the guys who spin around in washing machines and clothes dryers. Sometimes the clothes getting washed and dried are ballet clothes but usually it's in a different machine and most of the time it gets dry-cleaned anyway. In the case of Margot Fonteyn it's always dry-cleaned because she can afford it and it's cleaner that way and there's less detergent so the fish in the streams don't get croaked.

If trout could write they'd make up a big oaktag sign with the message "Thanx Margot for letting us swim out our days."

And that's just the point. Fish swim natural and they don't need swim instructors or dance instructors telling them how to move their fins and scales. Whereas human beings pay baseball instructors and ballet teachers such as the Kitty Carson Dance School (where guys are only allowed to take tap dance and only the gals are allowed to wear slippers) to show them what limbs to move where and for how long. But they don't tell them *why* to do it because there is no reason and if people knew there was no reason they would not do it but instead do something else like go to the movies or learn to sing.

Some people claim that Nijinsky learned a thing or two (well actually it was just one thing) when he was a baby from his nurse. She was a yogi breath specialist and somehow it's believed it rubbed off on him because he was supposed to have been able to stay up in the air an extra couple seconds and that means yoga. Levitation and weight reduction and he learned it from his nurse who never went in for ballet but stayed in nursing cause it wasn't in her stars so she never got to be mentioned in *Melody*. That's the picture with music by the Bee Gees and "Teach Your Children" thrown in for good measure and also some reggae bubble gum and it had a long run on 747's where you couldn't get off. There's a scene where the two young gentlemen get conned into a ballet lesson and the teach says "Think of Nijinsky, energy, *energy*" but they didn't think of Nijinsky and that's good for them.

Well the same could probably be said for diving cause they wear those silly *bathing suits* when they jump off the board to the tune of the beat in their head. The splash is all that makes it worth it but once in a great while somebody who dives turns out to be okay elsewhere and that's what happened with Buster Crabbe. Buster Crabbe turned out to be one of the most revered thespians the world has ever witnessed and he used to dive.

Some people say the same just might happen with another N-boy of the ballet, Rudy Nureyev. He's been to parties, he's been to Max's, he's been to people's houses and homes, he gets around and he's extremely popular and so lots of people are expecting him to do bigger and better things than *ballet* before his life is through. But he's only a star as long as the spotlight's on him and that can get mighty hot. But without it, like say he went to the Washington Street trucks after 11 PM, it would just be dark and he'd have to tell them his name or they'd never recognize him except maybe by his jumbo which, it's said, was once pictured in *Screw* but the picture was only 2-dimensional and most prods are 3-D so it still might be difficult. And it would be dark anyway so he'd have to tell them his name and they might not know it cause how many people can afford to go to Luxemburg which is the only city left where ballet is shown regularly? Not many so ballet may soon go the way of the dodo bird and the Brontosaurus Rex.

And another thing: ballet's as bad as ice skating.

# Bebop Confidential

REAL NAMES OF YOUR FAVORITE JAZZBOS RE-VEALED! Davego Scrom (Milford Graves). Sabu Hartnet III (Joseph Jarman). Wee Willie Toubadoux (Leroy Jenkins). "Fast" Axio Infanti (Steve Lacy). Abraham Bowelcartner (Dave Burrell). Gertrude Stuczynski (Carla Bley). Bayard Dutoetoe (Fletcher Henderson). Don't laff cause you'd change yours too if an unthinking mommy & daddy had christened you likewise!

*Jazz deaths this mo.*: Randy Weston (polio), Coleman Hawkins (smallpox), Chet Baker (suffocation), Cecil McBee ("natural causes"), Curtis Fuller (ulcerated prong). *At death's door*: Tommy Flanagan (heart disease), Illinois Jacquet (terminal scrotum cancer). Don't cry tho cause you gotta cash in sometime...

Bee bee *bee* buh duh *bee* bo bee bee bee bee bee—scronk—buh duh bee bee buh *deep* buh duh buh *doo* buh doopa dee boppa dee bee doo bo buh *dee* bee bee dee bo—honk—buh dee buh duh bee buh dee doopa *doop*. NAME THAT SOLOIST (hint: F-sharp clarinet).

Fats Navarro Junior ("Skip" to his friends, myself included) has finally entered the TWENTIETH CENTURY. "Broads are equal" announced the Skipper, not a musician like his illustrious pop, to an appreciative throng at ar the fourth annual Jazz Carpenters Convention in Duluth. Cookin with *heat*, Junius!

NICE DAY IF IT DOESN'T RAIN. Reading Popeye comics with those funny lookin hag people on an island named What? His sis was in the room; he didn't fug her. Watching the news is something they did not do. Green and orange motherflugging paper on the walls. Then it rained. Cats & dogs. Perturbed the *tuzz* out of alto man Giuseppi Logan (dropped a dump in his briefs). He fuckin *deserved* it.

*NATIONAL DIAL-A-JAZZ NO. IS (212) 999-JAZZ* so give em a call for a soundsational musical message (changed weekly). For Easter you could of rung em and heard "Mawanamabatawa-tanapatapa," Max Roach & Abbey Lincoln's profanely droll tribute to the city of Helsinki (known for its tin).

Jazz LP of the Month: None. Not a goddam one was released—first time since March 1960. Grachan Moncur's *My Wild Irish Arse* was due on the Afri-Koko label but legal problems and the cover getting fucked by the printers have shelved this recording for a least a fortnight. Too bad about the delay, as I'm told it's real "shit."

Arch critic Gary ("arpeggio in the 4th bar") Giddins of Gotham really gets my groat as the farmers say. He'd bore the trousers off Bob Iuliucci (you don't know him but he's dullll). Has been known to equate OUR MUSIC with "high art" as the Euros like t' call things and recently claimed "Ken McIntyre did not invent a sonic concept"—can ya believe it? CHALLENGE: I'm challenging YOU, Gary! to a battle of knuckle sandwiches, any time, any day, just name me when & where you want your FAT LIP and a nose like GEORGE CHUVALO and I'll BE there, buster! (Gonna fill my samwich with dimes & mayo so don't worry bout me, I'm being trained by Marion "Knockout" Brown.)

THIS MONTH'S JASS QUIZ: *Which member of the Pete Jolly Sextet has a daughter who is a retard?*

# Those Seventh Avenue Pushers

They're all over the place if the place is 7th Avenue or thereabouts in the 30's or so of New Amsterdam. Pushing and pushing and pushing varying stages in the production of what you and me and him will eventually wear and wear and wear. They're pushing so that we can wear, what would Mr. Marx say about that? These guys pushing their racks up the hill like Sisyphus, thousands and millions of times a day, every day. Well it's only five days a week but that's still 5/7 of the time. Why do they do it? Food, clothing and shelter is why, why'd you have to ask? You've had high school economics so you know the score.

As far as the shelter goes you know where they live: the ghetto. And the food: good enough to keep them alive so they can work some more. But the clothing is the weird part: they work so they can dress real neat, they're the spiffiest dressed members of the labor force in this or any other nation of the Western Hemisphere. Most of the threads they move around are worse than what they have on. So they know a thing or two too. They probably dress better than you or me. Better = more concern = more relevant to their situation as laborers in the world. They dress for work and the work doesn't require the usual togs so they can apparel themselves in *anything*. The nattiest work clothes from here to Kokomo. The workiest natty rags from here to Sinatra. Once in a while they must even be pushing around whatever they're wearing. That's like a guy who works in a library putting the numbers on the books and—by accident—taking out a book he's done the numbers for. Not exactly, because the pusher is per-petuating his own style of dress while the library guy is only hurting his eyes.

Ask a pusher why he does it and he'll give you an answer.

Tom Struthers, 22, keeps his mind on other things while he's pushin his blues away, soft things rather than hard. "You get to see a lotta fuckin broads on a job like this. You can even grab a little ass from around the fuckin rack while they're walkin by. One time I got me such a fuckin hardon I hadda hurry up and get back so I could pull on my joint in the fuckin bathroom. Those fuckin hot pants are outasite!" Nice work if you can get it and you can get it if you try.

Chico Morales, 20, just got out of the army. He enlisted when he was 18, good job-training there and he was so well trained that he's got this fantastic new job in the garment industry. Lots of room for advancement, the only way is up. Once a wheel broke on him and he still managed to drag it two blocks without anything falling off. Nobody gave him any congrats for the feat. After that he didn't care and he hasn't cared since. The test for department of sanitation is coming up real soon, he intends to take it. He planned to take the course at the Delehanty Institute that would've guaranteed him a passing grade on the written but he just never managed to scrape together enough scratch to take it. Or maybe he just forgot all about it. "My only regret is I didn't get sent to Vietnam and get wounded, you get a pension that way. I know somebody who doesn't have to work ever again and all he got was shrapnel in his arm."

Mel Sultan, 33, is nicknamed "Dumms" by his comrades and fellow pushers. He's not too bright, not that he's less worthwhile a human being, none of that: he's just plain stupid. He dropped out of Erasmus Hall High School and Erasmus happens to be in Brooklyn, where he still lives with his Mom and Dad. The hardest thing about the job is getting there in the morning. The subway ride into the city is no easy chore for him, sometimes he doesn't get off until he's hit the Bronx. He's lost a lot of sick leave on work missed by accident. Pushing is easy though, it's as easy as pie. He likes pie during his lunch break and sometimes he even brings some back in his coat for the afternoon. But why's he a pusher rather than, say, a janitor in a boiler room somewhere? "Um, uh, I like duh fresh air."

Ruben Valdivielso, 24, whose last name has been changed to protect his identity, has been pushing for 5 years and 3 years, respectively. 5 years of unbleached muslin and 3 years of horse and coke. And it's more than plurisignation which has brought the two most popular types of pushing together. "No puedo decirles cómo me siento realmente. El lenguaje que emplearía podría ser embarazoso. Creo que uno de los defectos principales del sistema que se emplea en la selección es que no fijan las cualidades estrictas que deben reunir los candidatos, entrando en la lista anualmente ex jugadores que a pesar de haberse desenvuelto con notoriedad y entrar en la categoria de estelares no son de los immortales." Loosely translated, Ruben is saying it's a matter of you're on the corner all the time, nobody's looking. Nobody's gonna notice if you hand something to somebody at a red light. Sometimes you have trouble spotting him so you have to catch him next time around. Occasionally the customers are co-workers and he feels real bad cause they're not making any more than him but he's not doing it full time so it's just a matter of pocket money. He's considered selling reefer but it's too much to carry around and the only thing he really feels like carrying is his radio to make the day musical.

Henry Ehrlich, 27, has a masters in history from N.Y.U. and he used to have a real soft desk job. He didn't like it. He hated it but at least he learned something about leaning on elbows. "Did you know that you have two elbows on each arm? Well it's true" mused Hank. "You're leaning on one elbow and, you're leaning on the *first* elbow on one arm that is, and it gets tired, your first elbow gets tired. So you start on your second elbow without switching arms. You know, it's a little higher up the arm, I mean it's a little further out. Your elbow's really two pieces and it has two points and they're joined by a straight line. The reason you generally lean on just one is that the one you lean on is the one that's more pointed. Well so you can switch off to the one that's less pointed, you can do it out of choice or just because you're getting too heavy on the original one. It might even *slip* onto the other one, in fact that's how I discovered it to begin with as something you could lean on. Like it's not easy to lean on it actually, you have to change your angle and your attitude towards leaning. And you can take the second elbow for about fifteen minutes and then go back to the regular elbow.

"You know when it's easy to rest on the second elbow? On the edge of a chair, you can lean it but then it's not really that easy to keep your hand under your chin holding up your head. Not that it won't take the weight, it's just sort of awkward and uncomfortable. But sometimes you don't even notice that you've shifted over to the second elbow because it's so minor but you usually do. You even got a third one too. It's further to the inside of your arm instead of outside and it's pointed in between, in terms of pointedness. But it's almost impossible to use the third one for leaning purposes but it's nice to know you got one." Why leave a job with so much opportunity for anatomical education? Uncomplicated answer: "Because I wanted to get more exercise than elbows and pushing a rack is good for your whole arm, both of them at the same time. And your shoulders. And your chest and the whole rest of you too. I'm in shape now and you hear all this talk about health foods and ecology and survival. Well a sound body needs exercise too and this way I have plenty of time to think anyway so it's the best of both worlds."

# Smack Is Worse than Downs

"Snorting smack is like 20 bottles of Romilar at the same time." So began Ed McCormack at the meeting of the Hot Tot Totsy Society. "It's like a lot of downs [he's right so far]. It's stronger than booze in case you're interested [right again and I won't interrupt him again] and it's an approximatin of what they bury corpses for, namely death. Which is great and the death part would be okay if you just kind of died the first time you did it and it was pleasant and easy but you don't and if you still want to then you gotta keep it up and what you're approximation then is the first hit cause you're not even allowed to just drift into the tomb cause you're too busy trackin down your next hit so it's a pain killer instead of a nullifier which is what it was to begin with. Nullification is great but then it gets to where it's a lot less general and a lot more specific and so if you wanna totally nullify the whole show you realize you gotta *resort* to something, you gotta actually take some action, drastic or otherwise. So it's like it's become movie-pitcher (sic) necessity and who wants to bother with that sort of shit if you're a junky and the possibility of total nullification is more remote than ever and it can't be as good as sleep no more." In other words to paraphrase the chump up to this point: smack is like when your girlfriend leaves you on the bus train.

And Easy Ed continues: "It's got the wrong hype both pro and con. They oughta go on TV and the radio and do the anti-smack ads by saying 'It's just like a bunch of downs' and if the kids like downs to begin with they're fucked anyway [c'mon Ed, whuddabout valium!]. Kids oughta start with smack first anyways so's they can go on to the other stuff from there. Acid oughta be next and then booze and downs if they insist and then the soft stuff like coke [sorry again Ed but how could you leave out nitrous oxide?]. The only thing smack doesn't do is sometimes when your body's nodding out your mind isn't and it doesn't wake you up when you're sleeping." Thanx Ed, even the inaccuracies were enlightening.

Yes smack is really outasight and sometimes inexperienced kids confuse the symptoms proper with withdrawal symptoms that they're always reading about so here's how to tell: it's the opposite of lockjaw where your jaws get locked cause your jaw just dangles, the lower jaw cause it's only hinged onto the upper teeth and not screwed on or anything, and it lasts about 16-20 hours and part of the time it itches but just in selected spots so don't chew your nails.

Cause if you chew em it'll be hard to scratch the itch and it'll just keep itching and keep you from getting a good night's sleep, with emphasis on the *good*. Sleep should be good because anything worth doing is worth doing well. So don't chew your nails off, you might get an itch in the eye. Eye itches are different from other itches. Eye itches are so vastly different from other itches that almost no comparison is substantial or happy.

And if you keep your nails in shape here's something you'll notice if you're right handed. You'll notice that there are two main ways to cut your nails on your right hand. You can have somebody else do it. Or you can utilize the lesser of your two god-given five-digiters, the left one. And you'd ordinarily think that your left hand's bound to have the best grooming than the right hand cause it was done by the right hand (i.e. the good one). NOT SO. It turns out that the right hand is the hand that gets the best cutting cause when your left hand is cutting it it has the *cooperation of the right hand*. Whereas the rightie doesn't have left's cooperation because left isn't coordinated enough to handle it. So like when the left is cutting the right it's the right that's actually doing most of the work and you'll also find that the nails on the right hand usually come off in one shot, you don't have to give each one two or three minor cuts before you get anywhere. It's true.

And they oughta recycle all the used nails and use them in natural backscratchers. With replacements for when they got worn down and you could buy them in either sharp or dull as you all know even dull ones get the job done too. But it's too bad that they couldn't use the cut nails for those fake nail products because nobody wants their nails looking like they're already cut.

# The Crow Flies High

The French scientist picked up the head and said the guy's name and the eyes opened and they moved around to follow the science guy around the room but then after a while they didn't anymore. So sez George Bishop in his very illuminating fuckin solid motherfuckin book entitled *Executions* (Sherbourne Press), the best book of the entire century, be they fiction, non-fiction, textbooks, biographies, autobiographies, cookbooks or plumbing repair manuals. What he's talking about is a head off a guy who just got guillotined for criminal acts against the state designated as a capital offense so they gave him a large sharp piece of metal in the back of the neck. But the head didn't die even though it was severed, proof that guillotines actually hurt. Which disproves the old theory that it didn't.

The first time they used a guillotine it was on animals to test it out and it worked okay on sheep and cows. But then they used it on a homo sapiens piece of horseflesh and it only went part way through cause it wasn't sharp or heavy enough so they had to raise it again and then a third time as well. Also there was this other time when the guy getting sliced had no hair so the executioner had to grab him by the ears to get him in place and in the scuffle the guy bit off the executioner's thumb as the blade was coming down! More than anything else in contemporary literature, this passage makes totally enthralling reading to the nth degree.

Same goes for when he describes the first electric chair electrocution. They didn't have any idea how much juice to pump into the poor sucker so they really *baked him to a crisp*! His brain was as hard as a brick when they took it out and his blood was black powder, and his face was reddish purple, and there was lots of froth and well-done meat! A lot like that similar scene in *Catcher in the Rye*.

The setting for the first gassing is the Old Southwest. The guy figured he'd never get gassed. So did the governor cause he had been the one to sign the bill into law that called for the use of gas to make guys dead. The reasoning behind his signature on it was that he figured there was no way to do it so the guys could never actually get knocked off by the state so—in effect—*capital punishment would be a thing of the past*! But he was as wrong as an owl in a treetop because they went and made him do it after all: they told him in no uncertain terms that he had better design and build a gas chamber or forget about being the chief executive of the state. So executive became executioner and they built the chamber and they gassed him and he didn't like that one bit. The governor didn't and the dead guy didn't and neither did his family and friends. His wife weeped and she'd be weeping on the pages right now if not for the fact that she met her own maker in the late 1940's due to spinal erosion. But the pages are very absorbent and you can put them thru a lot but it might be a good idea to oven-roast the book to soften the pages before reading if you are a hemophiliac who values your life because absorbency doesn't preclude razor sharpness at the edges. The surgeon general should insist on warnings about paper cuts on the bindings of all books but such is the publishing racket...

But then again this same racket has occasionally flashed with brilliance for allowing folks like George Bishop to speak their minds. And speak he does, in fact it's talk, talk, talk from first page to last and the talk is best when it's about ancient times. Like when Nero had this enemy he wanted to rub out with class. First he had the guy strung up by the hands and flayed for an afternoon while people fucked there who enjoyed the sounds of his vocal cords under strain. Then he got dragged out around the arena in the dirt with emphasis on aggravating the wounds to his person in the area of his skin. Skin has many layers and all were brought into play with consummate skill. The victim's, not Nero's. Skin that is, not skill. Nero's skill came in when it was time for the main event, however.

That was when they brought out the iron bull and they put the guy in it and put it over a fire at sauté heat. Whenever the guy made any noise there was some kind of thing that made it come out sounding like a bull, it had a lot of style. Meanwhile Nero had this Nubian sucking his cock and the last scream was real good, according to records unearthed by George Bishop, who could easily be vice-president of the Ace Fact-Finding Co. if he ever wanted to.

Like how many people are aware of the fact that England had this plan for croaking guys by injecting them in the arm with a needle? In the needle would be poison but the British chapter of the A.M.A. objected cause it would have to be administered by MD's.

# The Twelfth Swellest Town in Town

And it's not just because of its Purvin Milk that Wilkes-Barre (Pa.) is the 12th most all-around wonderful city in the United States. That's only part but it's much to begin with. Purvin Milk is manufactured only in Wilkes-Barre which is the same that can be said for Stegmaier the dwarf of beers. Yes Wilkes-Barre has both of em but you'll only get one at Krispy-Kreme. Krispy-Kreme is where they all hang out, everybody in town. They used to hang out at the mines but they closed down in 1947 so there's nothing left in this glamorous tank town but donuts and milk. Purvin Milk. It goes alright with donuts even though there's no cream in it, just milk. If there is cream in it it's hidden by homogenized but if there is cream in Krispy-Kremes it's hidden in them by non-existence. They're not krispy and they're not kremey and as a matter of fact Wilkes-Barre isn't worth the stay at any price unless you like the Steg. Some would say it's potable and some would not. I wouldn't. You wouldn't. Nobody would. IT'S REAL POTABLE.

But nowhere near as good as the Purvin. 400 U.S.P. units of vitamin D have been added per quart which makes it 100 per half-pint. And if they had 10-gallon hats in Wilkes-Barre that would bring the number to something uncountably high in the clouds. All the clouds in Wilkes-Barre are white, just like the milk, and the cow on the container is a lot fancier and simpler at the same time than either Elsie the Cow or the Crowley Cow on Crowley's Cottage Cheese and Crowley's Sour Cream.

And it's very good for keeping bodies in calcium that need it most, those bone-crushing denizens of the local gridiron that live in town and play football. Particularly for the kinds of special bodies they have in Wilkes-Barre (Wilkes-Bear?) (Wilkes-Barry?) (Wilkes-Bar?) with the very small heads on the very large bodies and long sideburns that come to a point that would be sharp if it was on a knife.

They don't use knives to cut the roast beef at the only Arby's in Wilkes-Barre but they use something mucho better. They use one of those electrical gadgets with the good blade that cuts every-thing paper thin. Well not exactly as thin as paper, after all you can't get a paper cut from it. Just imagine if you could get a paper cut from the Arby's roast beef, if you could you'd be bleeding and the blood would be tastier than the thin slop they supply at no extra charge in plastic squeeze-bottles. But there's no r.b. (get it?) (AR-BEES) cuts in sight and no knives for cutting, even of the plastic variety, so you are required to settle for the sauce and it's not even roast beef proper but in actuality *roast beef loaf* made from scraps left over from very dead bulls. It's no wonder bulls are getting mad!

# Do You Believe in Football?

Pigskin comes but once a year with its strange and amazing surprises galore so why don't we go and test our disbelief by taking a gander at the football division of Ripley's *Believe It or Not!*? Like what sane individual could have believed in his right mind that the Denver Broncos would blow it last year when it seemed so certain they were titlebound? I certainly didn't believe it. Nor do I believe Ripley's farfetched mind-boggler concerning Mr. Carlisle himself, the late great Jim Thorpe. It's the one that says he never called a time out. Never. I don't know.

But the one about Forrest Peters of Montana State kicking 17 field goals in one game (Oct. 29, 1924) is utterly credible, altho somewhat *dull*. The same goes for the business of Pee Wee McMahon (Trinity, Sioux City, Iowa) going into his first game with his first team and carrying the ball for the first time on the first play and scoring the first touchdown. It couldn't have been the first touchdown of all time so who the fuck cares! Then there's something about the famed and famous Bill Osmanski of Holy Cross: he carried for a TD his first play of his first college game and he carried for a TD his last play of his last college game (Holy Cross is a college). Now *there's* something decent.

Not exactly a horse of a different color is the oddity that occurred somewhere along the line in the illustrious series between Sacramento Junior College and College of the Pacific. Two touchdowns were scored after the final whistle. Just as the whistle blew T. Wilson intercepted a pass and scurried for a touchdown to paydirt. The play was ruled a throwaway and a washout because of interference and it was replayed. Again a pass was intercepted and again another touchdown was scored!

George Washington University completed 25 passes in 30 attempts and yet lost the game and not only that, they *failed to score*!!! No kidding, it's the truth, they lost to Roanoke 33-0. There must have been crying towels unfurled in the locker room *that* day!

Now here's an item you just will not believe, you just won't, it's just absolutely *incredible* but honest Injun I swear to St. Sebastian it actually happened: Joe Masnaghetti (Marquette University tackle) KICKED 3 FIELD GOALS IN ONE QUARTER (Milwaukee, Wisc., Sept. 23, 1950)!!!!!! Now let's see, seventeen divided by four is 4.25 so that other person kicked at least that many during at least one of the four quarters. But that's only if mathematics holds true for the physical universe and only if football is part of that same locale. Both facts are still as yet purely speculative, so...

Here's a good one: "A football game between Washington State and San Jose State—played in near-zero temperature—was attended by *only one paying fan* (Pullman, Wash.—Nov. 12, 1955)." They had thermometers then so why didn't they bother recording the exact temperature for posterity? Because there's a likelihood that the temperature might have equaled the number of paying customers on the nose (one = one)! Yes but that's no excuse for neglecting to record whether it was fahrenheit or centigrade, or even kelvin.

Now for some tales of imperfect bodies performing admirably even if the weather bureau flubbed *its* assignment. Ed Barrett had only one arm and yet he caught 4 forward passes and intercepted 3 in 1 game. That was when he squadded for Cedartown against Rome, Ga. He never played for Roanoke but "Rip" Patrone did, and "Rip" played an entire season with a *broken ankle*. Ripley doesn't mention whether or not the break was set (you'll remember of course that Kyle Rote once played the better part of a season for the N.Y. Giants with a *patched up* busted wrist in a cast) but maybe the similitude in the two names— "Rip" and Ripley— is responsible for his ungracious silence.

"Rip" was sure remarkable but he wasn't in the same league as D.H. Jeffries Jr., who played every down of every game in his four years of higher education. He was never absent nor late from practice either. Which is something that can't be said for Byron Haines of Washington, who scored all the points for both teams vs. USC. The score: Wash. 6, USC 2. Hubba hubba!

And: University of Oregon defeated the University of Idaho 27-21 without gaining a single yard from scrimmage (Idaho muffed it though by gaining 347 yards). Right: D.J. McNamara of St. Kilda, Australia, place-kicked a football 103-1/3 yards, 1907. Also: Dick Crayne of Iowa (not the same one who played Rocky Jones, Space Ranger) punted 102 yards, Iowa vs. Indiana, Nov. 3, 1934 (aided by the wind). And (yawn): Norm Swanson (Longmont, Colo., H.S.) scored a legal touchdown on his own pass. He threw it, it was fumbled by an interceptor, he recovered it and ran 44 yards to endzone glory.

But there are other achievements in sport that count as much as those by the nation's elevens. Such as those in badminton, where "Jess" (not *the*) Willard has been badminton champion for 10 years—yet has never played in a tournament! And those in swimming, where Clifford Thorne—Detroit—saved 1000 persons from drowning. As a reward he received one cigar. He does not smoke.

Okay gang, back to the grid again for one that's gonna wake you up even if you were born before 1704 (don't say I didn't warn you): Jabbo Stell (LSU) GAINED WEIGHT IN A FOOTBAL GAME! He weighed 168 lbs. before the game and 169 after it.

I'll repeat that one: HE WAS 168 POUNDS BEFORE THE GAME AND 169 AFTER IT. 168 minus 169 equals minus-1, representable as either a loss of minus-1 or a gain of plus-1. He gained a pound during the game, um, uh...wha?

The only possible explanation: he spent the game on the bench and spent all his time drinking water from the bucket and he never pissed. Or: the weighing was done with uniform *on* and he picked up some mud in the course of the action. Or: the scale was defective or the guy looking at the weights had defective vision. Or: somebody goofed in writing down the 168 before the game (maybe it was actually 178). Or: he sneaked into his locker after getting weighed the first time and ate half a mackerel before the opening kickoff. Or some combination of these.

# Frightening Blazing Tubes

Not all people are lucky enough to have walls to put their sets on. Which means the TV has to be on a table or a stool which means that some guests will have to be seated *behind* the TV. So they won't be able to watch it, right? Wrong, they can watch it by means of if somebody is seated so they can see it from the reflections in the people's eyes. But it may be a small image so have some binoculars handy. In fact even blind people can make themselves useful with their eyes for the first time in years if they simply sit where the reflections will do the most good and remove their eye patches or shades. But if the shades have a good reflecting surface then they should remain *on*.

Car people must have complained and maybe raised a big stink because the Bounty ad has been changed. It used to say "park that cup" and now it says "set that cup." Set it where? On the wet Bounty napkin product to show that even when it's wet it can still hold a cup. But if somebody was blind and they couldn't see then they might think (wrongly of course) that the ad alluded to a *car* being parked. And since the ad explicitly mentioned a *cup* then they might well deduce (wrongly again) that there's something rambling out of the Motor City called a Cup. And the wheels industry would not allow that mistaken conclusion to be propagated by the airwaves so it was changed to "set."

But where are the automotive people when it comes to the BP commercial? That's the one with Jack Kelly who used to be the lesser of the two brothers on *Maverick* (the greater of the two now looks like Fred MacMurray). He takes his finger and he draws a word in the dust on a car. The word is *thieves* without the I dotted. No dot on the I and why not? Because maybe it's the kind of dust that doesn't hold dots. Or maybe he's got a thing against dots so they should replace him with Billy Mumy. No they shouldn't, because that would lead to a conflict of interest suit with Dot Records, which has Billy under exclusive contract. That's the breaks!

CBS's *Your Palindrome and Mine* was scheduled as a regular weekly series at a reasonable hour for family viewing but some snags were encountered. Most notable of which was they apparently ran out of palindromes the first episode. I had a tape so I got em all down. Radar. Reviver. Able was I ere I saw Elba. Rise to vote, sir. A man, a plan, a canal, Panama. Murder for a jar of red rum. Wow. Nun. Bub. That was all they had and they apologized profusely but they should actually have given an apology FOR THE SIN OF LYING. They lied, there are actually two others which they failed to mention: 1. Are we not drawn onward, we few, drawn onward to new era?; 2. Tit I hit—ah what?—I hit it.

Educational TV's rerun of *Stan Getz Reconsidered* has drawn vast applause from music circles. Made up solely of films of his days as a man with a hole in his arm, it's got some grade-A footage. Like the time he played in Seattle and he could hardly stand up and he was wearing a suit which was soaked through to the air with sweat from his aching pores soothed over by the ravages of heroin. Then he and his golden tenor took to the mike and he played as good as Sunny Murray and Art Pepper put together. Sweden's gain is our loss and hopefully they'll be screening this show in Stockholm so he'll get to see it and come back home: we all miss you, Stan!

The fictitious Skippy of *Skippy the Bush Kangaroo* is sometimes played by a person. But only the person's hands when Skippy has to pick something up without use of his mouth. Kangaroos do not have prehensile paws like donkeys and coyotes and so a man was called in for the part. You could even call him a *stunt* man because not all stunts are dangerous. For instance it is not dangerous to drive in excess of 60 m.p.h. and yet it's still known as a stunt.

Channel 24 in Connecticut has this guy named Gionfriddo. He's Al Gionfriddo's cousin!! (The guy who made the catch against Dimaggio.)

Arlene Francis is now the only one left. Fred Allen died. Dorothy Kilgallen died. Bennett Cerf died. So Arlene Francis is the only one left. Now it's her and John Daly, he's still around too. But he's not any good, he's just as soon dead. She's good however and that's because she got her credentials early in the game: when she played that "lady of the streets" in that Bela Lugosi picture about the gorilla.

And *his* picture was on last week (*Bowery at Midnight*). He throws this guy off the roof *as a diversion* in a jewel heist! Wanda McKay tells John Archer "Why don't you try the millionaire's club?" and some other guy says "Why don't you run up and down Park Avenue?" Very, very, very good movie.

(Vicious rumor about the late Maurice Chevalier: he's reputed to have collaborated with the Vichy government, the National Socialist Party's arm in France. *Ja wohl vichyssoise!* As a result he is reputed to have reqested the American entertainment industry to fill his tummy after his countrymen caught wind of it after the war. You could call up the newspapers and ask them to look it up in their info service files but why bother?)

Stages are made of wood and boardwalks are made of wood and which wood is the sturdier? Well it's still up in the air because they held the Miss America Parade on the boardwalk at Atlantic City and it held the weight of the entire show and did not show any signs of collapse. Plus it even held up the weight of the audience and what stage can claim that? Let's see some stages with the balls to accept the challenge, yeah!

Right now Charmin has all the bucks so they can advertise their tissue for the asshole for removal of the accumulation of feces. But their toilet paper *doesn't compare* to Planet Facial Tissue with the attractive Saturn and stars design. It's not too soft, it's not too stiff. Its absorbency is just perfect and it's great for killing cockroaches. WHAT A SPECTACULAR IDEA!: if they ain't about to mention bowel movement on TV they could mention cockroaches because nobody but nobody uses it for their faces. Except to blow their nose and they could just as easily use a handkerchief or their fingers or sleeves.

The Taster's Choice ad with the middle-aged bald guy and his wife's nose job could have been avoided if he had taken inosotol and choline of the B-vitamin family. It prevents baldness and if he had prevented it it couldn't have been made using him. Unless they put one of those plastic head covers on his head over the hair, over the entire hair, but then they'd have to put some new fake hair on top of that in the fake spots where he's supposed to have it. It would be a monstrous waste of time and that's something TV doesn't have, time. So they'd never do it if he had taken his I & C.

Sylvanias have a rang dang doo of a name and no one knows

where it came from. A guess: he was in a pen in Pennsylvania and wanted to forget about the horrible times he had there, maybe it was even a pigpen which can be even worse. So he took off the pen(n) and but he should've realized that pork is the most intelligent edible animal in the animal kingdom and maybe he would have enjoyed himself and called it Swinesylvania.

# Those Pre-Code Tits

Funny thing about tits and non-underground comics. Given the usual sexist mammary mumbo-jumbo tits are just about the only indication that any hanky panky is going on at all. At least they're the potential for something like that or a constant reminder or something. Reminder of what? A reminder of the fact that if the stories were real-life situations (e.g. the one with Walt Patulski and his wife) there'd be lots of grabbing and feeling—and of course-a-dee-wourse some subsequent outright fucking and sucking. Guys just can't keep their paws off tits even when they restrain themselves. So tits are all there is in comics of *direct* sexual import if you get the picture. There's always the *symbolic* crap like sawed off shotguns as hampton wicks but that's indirect. And kissing don't count no more, it don't tip off a thing. One kiss leads to another and all that plop but Spider-Man's mask don't even have a mouth hole in it. So smooching's real far off in the corner as far as going all the way goes. So tits are the tipoff.

Before they brought in that Comics Code ballbuster there used to be a king's ransom in cleavage in every issue of every comic. But today you don't see that much except for when Steranko used to do Nick Fury and in the underground funzie-wunzies. That goes for both action and hints of action and bazooms too, which are sort of just shrunken remnants these days of the good old days before the mid-50's. And that's even though the statistics organizations are reporting that the knobs of the world are getting bigger by the month. And that's despite the fact too that people of the world are really bouncing those jugs around like they were basketballs. And meanwhile Lois Lane is more flatchested than she was all the way back in 1942 and it ain't because she's abandoned her bra and it's all hangin down!

There's at least two guys to blame for all these years and one's that Wertham character (the guy about how comics fuck up young minds), he was a real surly doodyface. But the real culprit is that fandango-monger John Goldwater who did the whole Code thing from his seat in the Archie building cause he was the publisher of

*Archie*! Gosh-a-mighty, particularly cause of all those many a male wads that have been shot over Betty and Veronica. But that's only a matter of adolescent butts-and-knockers under sweater and knee-length skirt. Borderline stuff and so imagination is required and since it's required a guy might as well just close his eyes and think about Queen Elizabeth taking a shit.

So for the real thing the only where to go is back to the old stuff which is now yellower than the stains would have been even if they dried up all the way ago. Stuff like there was this issue of *Pirate Prince* with a right nipple on the Black Mask who was female. It's just a black dot on a homogeneously green mini-dress before they were called that but there's five black lines that indicate creases under her paraboloid so it's some goddam dot. They got her tied up to the rack and her equipment is so impressive that one of her captors (he's goofy and bald with a bulging adam's apple like in the encyclopedia) unties her bonds. But she has to coax him a little extra by using her lungs for something else besides chest support, namely oral utterance: "Hello, cutie, you are the kind of he-man I can go for! Why don't you and I get married? We'll go away from this place and live happily on a desert isle!" Her legs are not especially appealing, in fact they'd look better on a horse so it's her pair that's doing it all.

Speaking of horses, there's a cowgirl with a pistol wearing blazing red breasts on a troubled stallion (the equine's eye indicates he just can't figure out *what's* coming off) and there's a cowpoke behind her holding on and he isn't even holding her well-molded fleshy parts as his six-guns flare to protect them from the rear. That's on the cover of a 1950 *Variety Comics* and there's no story inside that goes with it, it's just a come-on!

Those fuckers but there's three (count em) *Crimes by Women* stories inside, the favorite of gal's libber Lisa Robinson ("I know they're wrong but I love em"). One's called "The Big Money" and it opens with three broads backstage at the Club Flamingo and the trio's gotta be averaging at least 44 in the bust. And it's firm. Georgia the gorgeous blond bombshell has a red slip on thru which some nifty ass cleavage is visible. She gets a date with Danny Merrit, he's a drip and she's bored with him so she deserts the drip when his auto breaks down. Later on he shows up at her apt. pissed as all shit and he hides in the darkness until her shoulder pops out of her dress and then he slaps a big one on her mug. They become partners in crime and 2 weeks later she's still got a shoulder stickin out. But it's the other shoulder and another dress and Danny's suiting up with his shoulder holster and so chances are they musta been in the altogether just moments before. Therefore they both get rubbed out by the comic at the end.

Then there's *Jungle Comics* and in the heat-infested jungle scantiness of dress is kind of on the universal side so it don't indicate anything much at all in the comic. Tits ain't tipoffs and neither're the shoulders nor legs and all the swimwear's leopard-skin and two-piece. So the only sort of stimuloid stuff is cheesecakey model type shit à la centerfolds and classy angles. Frontal stuff gets to be a drag cause you seen one awesome cleavage you seen them all so the artist guys do downward shots and side shots for some new geometric prominence for the chest muscles. Camilla the jungle honey is in this one story with the Ape Witch. The Ape Witch has these two separate things for her knobs and a long flap over her snapper but the male gorillas she has with her *have no cocks*. Meanwhile Camilla herself's got a zebra top with one tit stickin out further than the other cause she's standing at an angle. So the protrusion gets magnified real good and the artist (name's Victor Ibsen) does some special shading in the cunt region of her zebra bottom. And he doesn't do any of that kind of shading elsewhere so it means: pubic hair snuck in!

Then there's one of the wicked Katomba (she's black with processed couture on her head) drawn from the back with more than a mouthful of bosom more than barely visible past her arm. Giving the reader more than was bargained for, a real peekaboo! She has the biggest combo in the whole book so she gets offed in a fire. And meanwhile the actual balling green level is kind of on the low tide in this one called "Captain Terry Thunder and the Congo Lancers" with the euroid Lion Queen Tawna leading an afroid tribe around her little finger. It's 1946 so she's obviously doing nothin with any of em—except a little domination—cause this is 1946 and the only way she's gonna be involved in any interracial gangbang follies is in retrospect.

There's also a Wambi the Jungle Boy smasheroo featuring a maharajah's daughter with a whip. They work the whip into the jungle setting cause she's an animal trainer/huntress. Her own epidermis gets worked into the eroticism by means of a plunging neckline cause royalty's daughters don't hang out in two-pieces. But if it's the urban part of town during wartime it's easy to get whips into the action cause there was plenty of torture due to jap and hun spies and the target was often women. On the cover of *Daredevil* #27 (the original not the Marvel) there's a good-looker of a bimbo with her face in pain cause her arms are tied to the chair and her foots are in boots and there's cement in the boots too and there's a masked meanie pulling her hair and he's whomping her mercilessly with a cat-o-9-tails (all nine have been drawn and you can count them if you wanna check). The men of torture are all naked as a judge from the waist up and her only coverage is slightly above the nips. Her lower limbs are good too and the guy didn't forget to draw a garter cause *comic stockings are sexier than comic bare legs*. But that's just the cover cause in the story it's her husband who gets tortured but the cover's enough to get scrods hot in anticipation of the guy's wife gettin it too but she doesn't.

Which for some readers must've been an unhappy ending. Which is the kind of endings love comics used to have. Narrow waistlines were big then and *glamor* was as high on the agenda as potential cunnilingus. All the chicks in those days were fully clothed at least from the waist up so there were no ribs to tickle fancies like in the jungle story pics. In "I Tried to Be Tough" in a 1950 issue of *My Story* there's this revealing nightie with spaghetti straps so you know she's not wearing any padding anywhere else in the story, cause it would show in the spaghetti. She makes out with John on the couch and he squeezes her real tight with his palms on her backbone so he could easily tell if she was wearing any rubber, proof in the pudding that it's the real McCoy. They *never* wear falsies in comics and that means they can never do the life story of J. Tiven's mum, she got one of hers nipped by cancer and now she wears some kind of a plastic in its stead. Medical comics could use her but they probably never will and that's a shame.

*Asses* are something else again and it wasn't till R. Crumb that they really got down pat. Except for Wallace Wood's asses in the early *Mad* which bounced with rumpular pulchritude in 1952. The Code eventually eliminated the original *Mad* so he ended up doing straightforward adventure type shit where there ain't that much opportunity to overstate. And that's part of why to begin with ass drawing never got off the ground: tits are okay as long as they're big but asses gotta have not just size but *shape*. The tit story was drawing both size and shape in unison was usually just too much of a bother but you didn't have to do it; but since the ass story called for *both all the time or forget it* not too many hacks bothered to begin with (hacks is what it's all about). Cause once you've eliminated one of the 2 essential ingredients in the formal structure of the female buttock you can just forget the whole fuckin thing.

So you get asses and *Mad* type parody shit intersecting the whole biz of the exploitation of distaffers as mere titties-and-rump: there's something *silly* and/or *funny* about well-sculpted ass in comics, it's a burlesque, a crude motherfucking put-on, a joke that overreaches those involving monster-size headlights. So it was inevitable for Crumb the bum to do a whole comic called *Big Ass Comics* of far-out fantasies with the behind in mind. He ain't ever done one called *Tit Comics* and it's too late now, tits are just too much a part of what it's always been about.

And speaking of about, how about arch hypocritical Mr. Al Kaplan who changed his name to Capp (a theory as to why: a cap can hold a tit in it) who's been minding the fronts *and* backs of womanhood for thousands of years. He's been knocking drugs and the nudity they bring but what about Daisy Mae? If she ain't nude she's far near it and she survived the Comics Code. Mammy Yokum survived the Comics Code too and she's always been well stacked, they're round and, yes, *nice*. So send Al Capp your bra filled with dead goldfish. 5% of American women have a third nipple but it's usually undeveloped but if it isn't and there's three cups to the over-the-shoulder boulder holder then fill the third one with anchovies from a can.

# Philatelicatessen

The psychedelic and philatelic movements have a fuck-tuck-tuckin helluva lot in common in case you were led to believe otherwise. Both movements hate the United States and all it stands for. One of the things it stands for is ugly stamps, for instance that hideous rendition of the youth of America on the commemorative that Eisenhower put out to honor American teachers in 1957. Also it does not honor its most important citizens: Babe Ruth has never been on an American postage stamp of any denomination even though he's dead and buried! They've even put out a stamp honoring the 200th anniversary of the fuckin Revolution and it ain't even 1976 yet, wotta bunch of impatient clods!

Also the U.S. don't know what to do with its colonies. England and Portugal do and France too. They put out some real beauts in the small perforated paper field with glue on the back in their colonies. Even better than the ones they do for themselves back at home to carry their own mail. And the more colonies the better cause that way there's so much work they don't do whole new designs for each different place but instead they have patterns that they repeat throughout the whole shebang. Patterns means repetition and that's the point! That's what stamp collecting's all about!

Plus they want their colonies to bring in some moola from the collectors of the world so they gotta make em look good, like with Cape Verde for instance, Portugal has to make the stamps good cause the name alone won't carry it, or even the location (a group of islands in the Atlantic Ocean and right after Cape of Good Hope in the album). The only money the U.S. is makin off of Puerto Rico is from rum and baseball players when it could be supplying stamp collectors with some fine stuff to someday pass on down to their children.

Plus the U.S. is rigid about what it puts on its stamps in the way of noms de country, only one name in various guises is ever used. So there's never anything really thrill-provoking like

Fezzan-Ghadames, Rouad, Ascension (altho there is a made-in-America recorded music event of the same name), Bahrain, Memel, Azerbaijan, Transcaucasian Federated Republics, Central Lithuania (Litwa Srodkowa), Penrhyn Island, Malagasy Republic, Fiume, Alaouites, Brunei or Bosnia & Herzegovina. But it's a good thing they never have had an American stamp with the B & H logo on it, a good thing for the U.S. stamplords cause they'd get sued by B & H and it would look bad on the internat'l law front. Particularly when Bosnia and company have that real mean looking bearded fucker on that brown stamp (he's real mean looking so he'd be merciless with transgressors) with the K-u-K-MILITAR POST inscription reminiscent of Amerikkka's own organization of the similar name.

Take the u that's there instead of the K and put them together and it's U.K. which used to have King George on all the stamps even though he looked worse than Michael Redgrave, what a fuckin shameless way to run a monarchy! Elizabeth herself these days looks really hideous from the left side of a 3/4 pose on such stamps as Cayman Islands.

Nor does the U.S. have a stamp honoring the oldest man who ever lived, Javier Pereira (1789-1956) who lived to be 167 and he's on a Colombian stamp (Columbus discovered America and they didn't even name the country after him!). No respect for age.

Nor does the U.S. have any decent fakes or counterfeitings like they once did with Croatia. Croatia folded in 1945 and yet there's some stamps circulating around honoring the 75th anniversary of the U.P.U. (1874-1949) which came out in 1949 or were supposed to of. There's buses on it and planes and other conveyances for the mail and the lettering is even fucked and the colors are blue and pink. Blue and pink, did you ever hear of anything so funny in your life! Come on, three cheers for whoever did it, you gotta show some enthusiasm for inauthenticity so take off your hat right now and put it to your heart cause the guy's most probably dead cause 1949 was a long time ago and he must've been at least 20 when he did it (or else he's a *genius* and so then you gotta *really* hand it to him). And if he's dead why hasn't the U.S. issued a stamp in his honor yet? Even if they don't have his picture they can still do a stamp with a likeness of his Croatians and a space for his face like *Esquire* did with the Rubber Dubber.

And the greatest stamp ("and the greatest stamp") that there ever was ("that there ever was") is a pretty little stamp ("is a pretty little stamp") from way Down Under ("from way Down Under") and on this stamp ("and on this stamp") it says PRODUCE FOOD! ("it says PRODUCE FOOD!") and it's red and white ("and it's red and white") and there's beef and butter ("and there's beef and butter"). And there's a third one in the series with a salute to wheat and all the plate blocks in the U.S. don't even have plates on them!

But the similarities between the psychedelic and philatelic movements isn't just negative, there's something positive and that's Tannu-Tuva. The best thing you can ever do for somebody who's tripping is put a copy of the Tannu-Tuva diamond in front of him with the airplane flying over the dragon and the skies are full of the *strangest* shapes! Blow your mind! He'll think he's hallucinating but such a stamp really exists and if he wants to be convinced cause he thinks he's losing his mind you can show it to him in the Scott Catalogue, it's for real!

# No Boobs at the Troub

And speaking of people who are nobody's fools, how about that former fatso who is now an ex-Monkee, none other than Mickey Dolenz? After all wasn't he the one who walked into the bar at the Troubadour (the one in L.A., not the one in Houston) and said "It looks like the first ten rows of *Let's Make a Deal*"? Yeah he was the one all right and meanwhile John Kay was there without his shades and Barry McGuire was over in the corner playing his axe over the noise and taking requests. Hank Frank of Hank Frank & the 5 Hot Dogs went over and asked him to play "Dawn of Correction," that song the Spokesmen did as an answer to Barry's "Eve of Destruction." Barry's response to the request for "Dawn of Correction": "Never heard of it." Could be. It was on Decca.

Decca's not half as good a label as Mercury. Mercury has this great album called *What's in This Life for You?* by Giant. I don't know if they have it anymore but it was out last summer. Did I say *out*? I mean it was around Mercury's office and storeroom last summer, I don't know if it ever got to the store or if it sold anything. But it's got the best cover in rock and roll, much more than you'd expect from just another 8-man band. There are eight of them but I have no idea what they sound like, I ain't never played it. The cover's so good there's no reason to rip the cellophane on it, that would only ruin the tension that keeps the whole thing so shiny and new looking. The cover itself has this big green terrier animal with red-rimmed eyes eating a red-haired sweety with swell gams and boss lipstick and ripped dress. There's drool dripping down the dog's mouth and it's pretty awesome indeed. It's Mercury SR-61285 in case you wanna buy it. Go buy it, or if they don't have it ask the man to order it direct from Mercury (212 245-3000). Go ahead, come on.

# The Cap Collector's Handbook

Tell ya what I just did. I just went thru my minor brands of soda cigar box full of bottle caps and fished out all the Costa caps and all the Clicquot Club (pronounced klee-ko or klik-kwat or however your lips feel like doing it) caps. They used to just be in the pile with all the other unsorted minor brand soda caps, now they're in their own plastic bags. All the Costa stuff (pineapple, birch beer, grapefruit) is in one bag, all the Clicquot stuff (lime rickey, orange, orange regular rim twist-off, orange high rim twist-off, sparkling water, imitation strawberry twist-off, tropical joy twist-off, root beer twist-off) is in another. All the Clicquots are from the West Coast except the fat rim orange (Manhasset, NY) and the sparkling water (Rochester, NY). The regular twist-offs are different from the regular regulars in that they have smaller eskimos cause the "turn off" lettering and the arrows that tell you which direction impose upon the eskimo trademark from the edge of the cap. The Costa caps are all bottled in Newburgh (NY).

Categorical decisions are a real big deal in cap collecting, even extending beyond the standard post-finding mere-categorical move to decisions involving the act of picking em up originally. Like you gotta think about whether it's a new one or one worth saving even if it's not: a singles/doubles convention which is yours if you want it. Which leads to stuff like: why have a doubles convention at all (within either/both the act of acquiring and/or the act of eventual differentiation into separate cigar boxes distinguished by varying *quality* of samples, and hence why have a quality differentiation convention either, etc....)? And why not extend criteria for uniquehood if that's what it takes to cut the mustard? Which boils down to do you wanna pick up *everything* (given sufficient pocket space) or just utterly new stuff or better copies of stuff you already got or any of that? And do you wanna *keep* everything, even doubles/triples and up? And if you do, do you wanna make quality type decisions as to which copies are to be taken as the primary ones etc.? And then there's stuff in how you keep the stuff and differentiate the stuff you keep. How packaged do you want it? How neat do you want it? How ordered do you want it? How much revision of order do you wan͏ a bother with? And all that sort of shit.

The way I've been doin it so far is first they were all in one paper bag and then it was two cigar boxes (beer & soda) and then it was six cigar boxes (beer/wine/cider/mineral water; Pepsi & Coke & other stuff they bottle; other major brands of soft drink defined ad hoc as major like 7-Up & Canada Dry & Hoffman & Mission for no major reason; some minor brands at random in one; some other minor brands at random in another; doubles), then finally members of the same brand got into plastic bags together if there were a lot of them, then two or more of any brand was good enough to qualify for a bag.

Plastic bags get in the way of the hobbyist playing with the stuff in unobstructed bulk, but they're essential to non-cumbersome maintenance of categorization and the single/double check (like you wanna know where to look for something to see if you got it already, once the mere beer-soda distinction was sufficient for that but with upwards of 1,000 different caps you need more boxes and bags not just for space-at-all but for further-differentiated-space-for-convenience). But in dry spells when you're not picking up anything new for weeks you oughta dump em all out and play with em if you want, allowing for a really massive checkout and organization/reorganization when you get a whole new batch of new ones: new stuff plus new stuff in the context of old bulk all over again (not always guaranteed to be fun by itself, but new stuff makes it fun).

Paper lists are an alternative, but it's a drag to write it all down (all the info including as yet *unforeseen* info) like with a cap where minimal differences in the writing on the edge and the rim are gonna make for differences in cap per se like with the standard Hires Root Beer cap's stuff on the side (NEW YORK AMERICAN BEVERAGE COMPANY INC, COLLEGE POINT, NEW YORK 11356 WHSI: that's on one of em that has no HIRES written on the inside cork and has CARAMEL COLORED and NATURALLY & ARTIFICIALLY FLAVORED on the front in white; on another it's BOTTLED LOCALLY UNDER AUTHORITY OF THE TRADE MARK OWNER,

BEVERAGES INTERNATIONAL INC., EVANSTON, ILL. with 16 inside a crown on the side and HIRES on the cork in back and CARAMEL COLORED AND NATURALLY & ARTIFICIALLY FLAVORED in orange on the front; another has PEPSI-COLA NEWBURGH BOTTLING CO., INC, NEWBURGH, N.Y. P.C.C. and HIRES on the cork and CARAMEL COLORED in white and NATURALLY & AR-TIFICIALLY FLAVORED in white with orange on the lower third maybe as a sloppy printing job and maybe by intent; and there are differences in the darkness of the brown). But it's okay to check out a brand where there's a *limited* number of things to consider (you hope and you pray) by means of a check list: here a check list is a mundane obvious advantage out in the field in the heat of a cap hunt and back at the shack if you don't feel like digging into all the boxes and bags. But see if you can do away with mundane obvious advantages as often as you can when preferences for specific collection/categorization conventions are involved, like why not?

And plastic bags make for *monism*, man: if there are near doubles in a mere *pile*, the order of pulling em out affects your attitude towards the potential grouping (the universal in the universal/particular hogwash) as you pick em out one by one. You get a situation of those picked . . . those not picked . . . those not yet picked . . . those missed, the old completeness/incompleteness am-biguity. Why it's the same case in a bag, you'll say. But in a bag there are no large temporal gaps between caps of the same family unless you choose to do it that way. And in that case maybe it's cause you're taking it casual enough for it not to matter (it's a hobby) or cause you're bored/familiar enough with it all for it definitely not to matter (it's a drag) except as self-inflicted completion on your part (enslavement to the rigors of hobby). Or maybe it gets split up by answering the phone or fixing a cut finger (cut by a cap), the usual postulated pragmatic/aesthetic separation, so the return thereafter (if it *is* directly back to the same bundle under examination) is a move to that bundle as the *first* you hit—as opposed to getting to it after a while from within a larger super-bundle (accidental heightened relevance move). Then there's your memory and *its* role, and your decisions as to where to put your caps up and down in a pile and whether to have em face up at any level, particularly (and not) on top. Then you have stuff like visual outlook for the present or any future present (in terms of what you feel like seeing right away and what you feel like *planning* in terms of that) and visual outlook in regards to possible damage-enhancement to the surface appearance of individual caps (and how much mere prevention you're interested in if any and how much you know in advance about the lasting power of the finish of different caps and how much you learn and regret after the fact) due to juxtapositional moves with piles and packages.

Time for some differentiae. Of course you can go around during days of low pickings and pick up lots of minimally new caps like the Hackensack NJ version of the same old 7-Up and the Hoffman Ginger Ale with smaller letters, you can do that you know, it's just like collecting postmarks if you're a stamp collector and you wanna extend your pickings when they're low. But with caps you don't have to say you're collecting geography (like you'd have to admit to yourself with the postmarks: you'd have to say now I'm a postmark collector *in addition to* a stamp collector): you're just collecting caps! And minimal distinctions are much more plentiful in caps than perforation differences or watermarks in stamps.

But let me caution you that this is no unwarranted casting off of all limitations. No, no, not at all: like collecting *requires* limitation, like if *anything* can qualify then what's the difference whether this or that or whether you even got it or not or stuff like that. As far as caps go, twist-offs bring up definitive limitation. Originally these bulky items served only to increase the size of a collection sizably cause they were *around*, you could find em easy, you could agree to say they were okay, etc. But if you extend beyond beer and soda twist-offs you get into the realm of that massive bulk of extra-soda/beer ordinary mundane *all-caps*: Mott's Apple Juice, Seagram's 7, Sau-Sea Shrimp Cocktail, etc., all that stuff. So you gotta sort of go back to the primal cap (you know what it looks like) and start from there and say that even soy sauce caps are okay if they're *shaped* right. And once in a while you get into controversy about something like the Poland Water twist-off, which is the twist-off extension of what's originally shaped right all right, but this twist-off itself is shaped mighty *funny*. So it's up to you what you wanna do with it if it ever comes into your possession, if you ever let it come into your possession (*I* would).

Then there's the makeup of the liner of the cap. It can be cork, cork with a circular metal thing, plastic, rubber, paper. And the plastic liner being taken as constant, there can be variation in the design thereto affixed (which may actually even have relevance in determining how tight it seals): it can be round with no lines thru it, round with one, two, four lines thru it, concentric circles and so on. One Canada Dry twist-off (Canada Dry presents some bummers because their twist-offs are all the same for all flavors and they don't indicate the flavor differences in any way on the caps, you gotta look for other distinctions in order to build up a sizable Canada Dry collection, but there's always the possibility of keeping and labeling all unlabeled caps as exactly what they are so you can have visual doubles that are *labeled* as different, but then you'd have to account for stuff you find unattached to a bottle and that would lead to a hard ambiguity to live with but once you know about it it's always there anyway so it's too bad now that you know) can show up with lots of different liner designs, Schaefer is big on that too. And there's lots of different pictures on the back of Coke all the time, Disneyland and famous explorers and stuff. And Yuengling Beer (Baltimore) has different numbers on the plastic and who's to call em not entirely different? Depth of the liner counts too, sometimes you gotta scratch it to test it, particularly if it's all bent (some of the best stuff is best cause it's bent: I got a Rainier Ale cap bent around into a full cylinder and a Sunrise Orange cap with the upper half bent and scratched into a sunrise by tires and feet) so you can't easily judge it with just the naked eye. You can use a nail. You can use a nail file. You can use a nail (metal).

And sometimes nasal identification is important. Like when it's foreign or something so you can't tell what it is in terms of beer/soda except by sticking your nose in as far as you can. Even after it's in the box with all the others for a long time it still retains its own smell. An unidentifiable cap of mine (all scratched up and rusted) once turned out to be just another Champale after smelling added onto one minor visual hint (2 legible parts of letters) gave it away.

Some caps, particularly on the West Coast so far, come in the pull-off variety, like the Rheingold Chug-a-Mug only smaller (the size of a regular cap with the addition of a puller). Bet you'll be surprised when you see Dr. Pepper in a pull-off (if you haven't seen it already).

And there's variation in which *bottling company* did the cap too, which can also lead to categorical ambiguity/duality moves (good) like whether a Mission cap done by Plaza Beverages should be filed with other Mission caps from Boston Beverages or with Big Giant Cola from Plaza (or is it just *bottled by* Plaza *in this particular instance?*) and whether a Titan cap (Mexico) oughta stay by itself or with Orange Crush since it says HECHO EN MEXICO, ORANGE CRUSH DE BAJA CALIFORNIA. Makeson's Stout and Whitbread Ale offer the same problem if you can call it that. Etc.

Okay it's time for a cap hunt! The best place to make a real killing is a faraway hick town with a few gas stations; tourist hick towns have more gas stations than regular hick towns. You take along a long flexible piece of something that's stiff enough but bends enough too and you stick a wad of gum on the end and stick it down the pit under the opener on machines that sell bottles. The best kind is the one that has the bottles horizontal and you can pull em out and you get a view of not just the type of soda but the cap itself: you can use your opener (always carry an opener) to get the cap right off the bottle without buyin it, the machines protect against taking out the bottles but not against cap removal. Anyway you can fish for the unknown by sticking the gum thing down into the thing and gettin em out one by one—and sometimes two and in rare cases more. How cautious you have to be in removing it depends on how deep it is and how sticky the gum is. Last summer in Solvang (Cal.) I picked up about 25 different caps from the machines of five gas stations, including an entire set of Bar-B (root beer, strawberry, grape, orange, if that's indeed complete) and some LA Patios you can't find in NY (strawberry's one of em). If you're thirsty you can always *buy* the stuff (summer's good for that), and it's good to have an opener with you for just such a case: first you might lose the cap down the pit and not wanna fish for it (like what are the chances of catching *it* on your first shot at it if you don't happen to grab it as it's coming off the bottle?), and then you might prefer to remove the cap your own way (as by sticking the pointed end that you use for beer under each thing on the rim of the cap and pry it off slow-like: that way you don't bend the main part of the cap, altho you might prefer to have it that way or you might not want the original angle of the ridges on the rim interfered with). You might even go for an occasional machine type bend however, or you might not wanna carry metal around with ya, it's *your* move. And sometimes the best gum for stick is stuff you find lying around.

Supermarkets are the best places for getting twist-off caps free. You just twist em off when nobody's looking. The high rim twist-offs are a little harder to get off cause they're attached in a few spots, the regular rim twist-offs (you can't always tell which ones are twist-offs among the regulars, you hafta do some reading, they're less conspicuous than the high rims, *all* high rims are twist-offs) are easier and you can get a better grip. And if you have your opener along you can even snap off some non-twist caps, only you'll probably get forced to snap em off quick so you can't do the slow deliberate non-bend job. If you rattle the bottle while you're doing it the stuff'll fizz up, particularly if it's warm, so watch out, that might attract some attention if it bubbles out and drips all over the place. But even if you've been fingerprinted they're not gonna check the prints on the bottle with the FBI to find you out—not yet anyway. And not buying the stuff pays off doubly with items like diet swill (even without cyclamates) and bummer beers, you don't have to drink it or pass it on or dump it out and feel like you wasted your money. Once in a great while you'll find a broken bottle in a store with a cap still on it that you need: you can stick the whole busted neck in your pocket and remove it later, you can remove it with an opener first, or you can get it off without an opener by smashing it against the ground enough times (but that's a good way to do it any time, unless you wanna get a deposit back, but deposits are going out the window anyway, recycling to the contrary).

Then there's always city streets and hot dog stands and those cardboard boxes that the guys in stores stick under the opener they supply for purchases. In the street sometimes you gotta dig stuff out of the mud and stuff like that to get at and sometimes you hafta do it just to get a look at the rim or the back on the chance that it's a new one even if the front's the front of one you already got. And if it's stuck in the pavement cause the pavement's hot or cause a car flattened it in there an opener is often helpful in digging it out. And it always pays to keep your eyes to the ground wherever you go, no telling when you might find something, it's a good habit to get into. Also, it pays to influence relatives and friends to buy stuff with caps you're after, and be sure you're there when the caps come off or you might have to fish thru the garbage. And if they replace the cap on the bottle cause the drink isn't finished make sure you follow the cap's progress to the moment of its final disposition. And drinking some of it helps speed things up and you can always spill it out little by little or just snatch the cap when nobody's lookin, it's a real setup cause you don't even need an opener (just your fingers unless it's on pretty tight) and nobody will make you pay for it if they find you doing it (particularly since part of it's already been drunk), they'll maybe just get mad at you. Anyway, it's a good idea to interfere as boldly as you can with the drinking and opened-drink retaining habits of your crowd, but not too bold as to mess up future operations.

Something I've been wanting to do for a long time is reopen the Alt Heidelberg case. Is it a different cap or isn't it? The carton says it's Alt Heidelberg and the label says the same but the cap calls it Imported German Beer (that's enough of a name for the standard American beer slob and, y'know what, it's a good beer) and I have in my possession *two* quite similar Alt Heidelberg caps, the only discernible difference being the amount of space taken up by the word BRAUEREI on the edges of each. One is (or could be) bigger, the word on one of them. So they're different! Yay!

Did you know that the first soda in cans, the late great Super-Coola (originally only in Cola and eventually all flavors of the rainbow including a real good lemon-lime), had caps? Yeah you needed the round end of the opener to handle it (unless you opened the cap with the pointed end for obvious reasons) and you didn't even waste the soda if you didn't feel like finishing it in one session: you could cap it up again. Nehi was a few years later and that was just a can, altho you can now get Nehi in bottles with caps on em! But I'd give my left leg for some Super-Coola caps right now, if you've got any stored away and you're a nice guy why don't you send a few over to a guy who could really use em, I could really go for em in a big way! And if you don't have one of them but you drink regularly (or even if you just notice caps all the time lyin around in the gutter) anywhere in the world, please send me some, please. I'll become your pen pal, and if you have nothing to mail them in I'll be glad to send you a cigar box (there'll even be some cigars in there for you). You can reach me at the following address: Richard Meltzer, Box 85803, San Diego, CA 92186.

I'd really appreciate hearing from you!

The whole thing's easier to show you than write about: when you're in town, come on over. I'll show ya around and what's more I'll let ya see the caps (an open invitation to the people of the whole world). I could have been clearer in the cap writin I just done but I had to spend my time tending to my caps. You understand.

My favorite cap? Well I guess that would have to be the Three Horses Beer cap I picked up in an old whaling village by the name of Stonington. It's real cute, three horses each with a different expression. But that's just my favorite *neat* cap and my favorite cap for *content*. Otherwise it's gotta be the one I found in Berkeley that was all rusted and is shaped like a *cap*. It has a peak like a baseball cap so you can pry it off like that. Only you can't read anything on it so there's no telling what it once was (the smell test doesn't help cause it smells like rust), so if you have any info on it let me know, okay?

# Hoops Among the Bubbles

The printing job the Topps bubblegum people did on the Connie Dierking basketball card is so gosh awful horrendous that a number of crucial numbers are not visible. That can be crushing if you don't know your X's and Y's but if you do there's nothing that can prevent you from constructing the entire picture of Connie's fab career as told in numerals. In the free throw column the card reads as follows:

$$83$$
$$108$$
$$114$$
$$lab$$
$$c50$$
$$1de$$
$$237$$
$$243$$
$$\overline{\phantom{0000}}$$
$$1069$$

No there's no letters in it, those are just to indicate where stuff is missing, like the lab means it's a hundred and something, etc. So by totaling everything up in each column you get the equation $25 + b + e = 29$ or $39$ (it could be either), so $b + e =$ either 4 or 14. In the second column it's $21 + a + d +$ either 2 or $3 = 26$ or 36. For the hundreds column it's $8 + c + 2$ or $3 = 10$. It can't be 3 because that would make it 11 in the total, so it's 2. So $c = 0$. So it's 26 instead of 36. Therefore it's $a + d + 2$ or $3 = 26 - 21 = 5$. And $a + d = 5 - 2$ or 3. If $b + e = 4$, then $a + d = 5 - 2 = 3$. If $b + e = 14$, then $a + d = 5 - 3 = 2$.

Meanwhile from another angle it's 536 in the points column for the 64-65 season, that's the year of the lab and there's 218 field goals that year too. So it's $536 = 2(218) + x$, so $x = 536 - 436 = 100$. So $a = 0$, $b = 0$. Then since $a + d = 3$ (because $b = 0$ and therefore $e = 4$, it can't be 14 because it's gotta be a one-digit number), $d = 3$. So $1de = 134$. And $c50$ was just plain 50.

Did Connie's 70-71 play merit all the archaeology involved in dissecting his previous seasons? Yeah because it couldn't have been worse than the season of that so-so 50 free throws, that was the year he averaged a stocky 5.6 all season.

# Grappling's Cascade of Blood

In sunny Calif. they call it lucha libre and what it often means is two grown up adults (but midget and dwarf adults are allowed too) wrestlin on the dirty side of the fence. Any place that's also the boxing capital of the USA as far as amount and intensity of activity is concerned is bound to also have a lot of mat activity that's even better.

Better because it's got none of those preferences regarding such nonsense as staying vertical. The mat's where the action is and not just the feet and their footwork. All over the world and especially in LA where every fight has at least one Mexican and they beam it over to New York on channel 41. When Fabulous Don Carson made mince meat out of The Masked Toro with a series of mean knees to the mid-section off the ropes in 2 straight falls he demanded the mike. "I ain't gonna speak to you guys in Spanish so if you don't know English you better learn it cause I ain't gonna talk your language to ya!" And he wasn't being educational when he said it. He was an ogre and all ogres teach you is eat or be eaten.

But Toro looked pretty rough and tumble himself and could have won either of the two falls. In the first he got thrown through the ropes sure but he lost no time in applying a crushing headlock on his giant foe. A tug broke him loose but a flying knee lift knocked Carson flat once more. Body slams were exchanged and followed by knee drops to the head rather than the neck or chest. Head work can take its toll faster than a belt to the starch and for one fall at least Toro's shoulders remained on the canvas for a full count of 3.

Speed and style seemed to be getting the best of strength and ferocity temporarily at least. But suddenly Toro, moving with a swiftness that belied his poundage, seized Carson in a bear-hug The 6'2" Carson looked like a dollboy in the mighty paws of a large elephant. But which one was fatter it wasn't easy to ascertain. Lack of uniform uniforms was responsible. One guy had a big tub and it stuck out between his mask and trunks. The other had a full length thing with upper thigh slits but no indication as to whether or not there was a corset holding in his ponderous abdominous if he had one. And I'm not claiming he does. But at least PROFESSIONAL WRESTLING permits lard, which is honorable and you should allow it too. Kiss a fat man today. Same for tall people, kiss one of them.

In another match former circus aerialist Judy Grable yelled "Leggo my hair" at Fran Gravette, then wound up and slugged the hapless Fran with a hard right that was also powerful. High-flying fireball Grable—no relation to starlet Betty—hoisted Gravette to her shoulders and prepared to flip her out of the ring but Gravette wrenched loose and the two hellcats broke into an extended free-for-all! Yowees! But the Fabulous Moolah remains superior to the both of them and she may DIE the champ.

Viva Las Vegas!

# The Red Nappies

Before the end of this decade the Asbury Park Convention Center will no doubt witness the world's first Miss Wonderfully Beautiful Pre-Pubic American beauty pageant or the equivalent. Betty Bunds'll be standing there under hot lights in her yellow 2-piecer getting asked "Betty how many brothers and sisters do you have?" As she answers "Four or five" an unfamiliar moisture will sparkle twixt her young hams. Without a flinch the smiling host's gonna then come back with "Well how many is it, four or five?" as scarlet dots the yellow you know where.

Straining to retain her cute little composure she will break into a blush as her lips mouth "It's really four I guess, cause one's dead" to the laughter of millions of delighted tviewers. Meanwhile all the live beauty lovers in attendance will gasp: BETTY HAS JUST MENSTRUATED FOR THE FIRST TIME!!

So maybe it's about time tampons were made part of the regular costume for these events. The only other possibility is give the kids birth control pills to prevent bleeding internally even if it's never happened to them before. Cause it always *could* happen right then and there for the first time. The only other alternative is a total revamping of society's outlook re crotch blood, make it into "blood is beautiful" cause it *is* of coarse. But it ain't gonna happen within this decade, which is the deadline for the pageant so it's gotta be the tampon alternative.

Cause sometimes there's bleeding even with the pills. And the bathing suits they're designing these days just ain't absorbent enough to hold back the flood and it'll be dripping toward the knees within seconds. Napkins could do some of the absorbing but they'd make her look like she had a cock and balls or a napkin. And napkins are as obsolete as life insurance so why do they still try to sell em?

Nobody but nuns and the elderly and infirm use those kind of rags anymore but they do use Tampax and they use it well. The largest selling and most popular of the plunger type gadgets for that time of the month in every woman's life, its name has become synonymous with the whole show in tampons, which have just received their first moments of glorious publicity via the airwaves and God bless em. In the case of Tampax altho the inserting apparatus is made of cardboard it's not rough. You get good diagrams with the box. It's cheaper made than tampons that you have to insert without a plunger, but only because you'd never be able to get them in if they were made like Tampax cause the shape is not solid and they spread apart. Like if they ever came out of their plunger it's almost impossible to get them in.

Meds are no good, they have a plastic plunger that's supposed to be soft like your body. They're supposed to conform to your body but the initial feeling upon insertion is *scratchy*. It scratches you and it's not bio-degradable down the bowl like cardboard is. It even seems like it could get caught in the pipes and clog things up. It's too well constructed for its own purpose, another piece of plastic in the world that isn't what it's supposed to be.

Then there's the ones without a plunger and if you're at all squeamish about how far you think it should be in they're no good but they have one definite advantage over the other ones cause a package of 10 or 12 is no bigger than a box of cough drops. But there's big boxes of 40 too. Pursettes is one and it fits in a purse if it's a small box. They claim to have a lubricated tip but it's like hard glue or something and you have to shove it in with your finger. It's really a hard solid thing rather than a soft piece of cotton. You can send away for a case that holds 3 for 10 cents. It's not *that* bad but it's uncomfortable and it can be felt when you're sitting down.

Playtex tampons (hats off to the bra folks!) and Kotex tampons (pants off before you stick them in) both use the plastic too. You get 12 for the price of 10 with Kotex but the plastic is thinner than cardboard so it fits in a similar size box. Playtex boxes have flowers to look mod but Tampax is all business. If you take the cellophane off the large-size Tampax box you don't have any words on it except in the corner so you can keep it in the office and no one will see and it doesn't distract anybody from work.

Tassaway has those little cups that look like nipples and they're wider than a Tampax and they hold a whole day's supply of blood which can then be saved for cooking. Because of the size it presses against the rectal wall plus you have to push it in and sometimes it doesn't pop open. So it doesn't always collect in the cup, it doesn't work, it's useless. But there'll be more of them in use than napkins in two shakes of a lamb's tail. So those magazine ads with the little girl ready to be introduced to the magic of bleeding into a napkin are simply an anachronism. No one knows why the myth of the obstructing hymen lasted as long as it did but thank heavens it's all over now. Why there aren't enough cherries left in the entire country to produce one average-size cherry pie! But that's besides the point when it comes to tampons and Miss Young Virgin contests.

And they could even have them wearing compulsory Pampers at the shows because those would be virtually invisible cause they wouldn't be lumpy in one spot and they'd absorb it pretty good and not drip out. It's certainly not ecologically sound to have them instead of reusable diapers but beauty pageants should be exempt from those kind of stiff requirements.

But there's one thing that absorbent blood drinkers of all types can't do and that's prevent death due to hemophilia which the first menstruation brings to thousands of females annually (the percentage rate of death is far higher than sickle cell anemia). Some day (it's inevitable) one young miss will become a fatal young miss before the end of the event and her parents will probably swear on the nearest bible that they'll never have another child and wrongly so. Because there's every chance the next one might WIN the event in, say, 10 or 11 years hence so they oughta keep on trying. Winners never quit and quitters never win.

But what of the old distaffers in the population, are they to be utterly forgotten in the period department? No. There should be some effort day and nite in the development of a truly menopausal tampon that could be used for lengthy periods of time of, perhaps, ten months to a year at a time. It would be for after fucking has taken a back seat to dying and, consequently, the hole is of no longer use so it might as well be plugged up in case an unexpected sudden flow of claret should occur from out of the blue. A cork wouldn't work because it would probably work its way free due to constipation or a rough ride on the bus. And, besides, it's not as absorbent as canvas and could be used for a better purpose anyway, like bulletin boards. So the tampon wizards oughta get to the old drawing board right now (preferably not cork because their pencils would get stuck in the holes) and get one in the stores by 1975.

# Lose Your Appetite but Not Your Mind

If you were to tell certain music fanciers in the fall of 1964 that the Righteous Brothers were no more than the Everly Brothers version of Ray Charles you were apt to be stiffly argued at. After all what's originality got to do with flats and sharps? Particularly when fans are involved. Yet some would add the rejoinder that if a man can think he can dislike. And if there's any reason to dislike unoriginality then it will happen if you're so inclined.

So it is with music but what about candy? Candy is different because it's eaten instead of heard. It's easier to see and not hear than it is with music too. You can see the music getting played but you have to cover your ears or be on the other side of the glass to avoid hearing it. Not so for candy, you can look at it all you want without having to cover your mouth with gauze. And eating also entails the least amount of thinking per capita of any of the senses including balance. And scarfing candy is no difference.

So one way of looking at Wowies is that they're the Goobers version of M&M's but pop em down your maw and they're a whole new ballgame. When they're in there with the tongue and teeth and spittle you can't see em so they're eaten and not seen (15¢). If you could see the U.S. certified color you'd think you were inside a rainbow with all the pink and green and yellow (Myers) which do not go with any candies except Jordan almonds (Standard Specialty Company) so eating eliminates further speculation into the odious business of candy aesthetics (1028 44th Avenue) so enjoyment is possible (Oakland, California 94601).

Candy is like a toy and you know what? There's less ads for candy on TV nowadays than there used to and there's more ads for toys. Toys cost more's gotta be the reason why but candy costs more too (15¢) than it did then. But it's still cheaper than toys ($25) and it's more fun anyway and it's educational too and it doesn't even require a costly teacher in residence or the encyclopedia. And who ever thought a mouth could learn you so much?

Mouths know all the variables and they tell you about it constantly if you'll pay attention, you can learn regardless of whether you're 40 or 14.

To wit: the shell is tough (the candy coating on the outside is tough), the peanuts are sometimes salty (the peanuts on the inside that are small in comparison to the ones in M&M's and the shells are smaller too), the peanuts are sometimes stale, the chocolate is sometimes thin and there's less of it than in M&M's, the color on the outside can get licked off just like with M&M's (they tell you about not on your hands but they never mention your tongue) so they are not ideal sucking candies (but you don't have to look at the color while you're sucking so it works out A-okay despite the fact).

All that you learn and more. Eat a hundred boxes and you're a regular B.C. (bachelor of candy) and you'll need calcium to keep your teeth strong and healthy in the face of etc.

# Dribeck Isn't Jeff Beck

Beers have to have companies, it's a fact of brewing life that there's no circumventing. Heineken has a company and it's a good company that has Heineken's best interests at heart. Beck's is a horse of a different color even though both bottles are green. Beck's and Heineken's. They're both green and not only that when it comes to Heineken's, Heineken's has a GREEN CAP too. Heineken's regular is green but Heineken's dark is brown and Heineken pilsner is red and the ones you see in the city streets are mostly green.

Green because they come from a bottle of Heineken's. Two years ago they were beginning to appear all over the place just like Volkswagens in 1948. Before that there were only about point two Heineken caps per city street per year. Yet today there are more than twenty per block per *week* and if that ain't advertisin nothin is! Free ads and they don't even have to pay for them cause the streets don't charge for the ad space and people have to look down to avoid the dogshit on their new shoes. And people with new shoes drink the most beer (people with old shoes drink the most wine).

BUT BECK'S HAS A BLANK CAP! In this day and age! No writing on it at all, just plain silver like any other and take my word for it, there are literally *thousands* of silver caps extant with no words on them. Beck's is one of them and if they expect to get the gears moving on American sales they better bust ass to get the cap some colors and a logo before Xmas. Or else nobody's gonna believe it gets drunk by anybody, TV ads aren't gonna convince a soul. Just cause it's #1 in Germany don't mean Americans of non-hun lineage are gonna cotton to its special slurpability. So something's gotta be done with the caps and soon. But the past can't be recaptured so all those silver caps in metropolis gutters right now are lost to Dribeck Importers, Inc.

But here's a way out of the maze: start an ad campaign featuring the blank silver cap exclusively instead of the label on the front.

That way people would think everything silver's a Beck's cap and they'd go out and buy some themself. Caps are good for companies. Companies should be good to caps.

They sure should.

Sure.

# Wearwithal

It seems like only yesterday they had that first arrest of a young lady in Racine for wearing one of those already famous (altho unworn) Rudy Gernreich one-piecers. It had more material than both halves of a two-piecer put together and yet it got to serve as a paradigm for the obvious (obviously totally nude for at least a while) future. Faulty approximations aside, there were not too many more arrests à la Racine and it turned out that fashion was the flimsiest possible context for individual topical reiteration, or so it seemed.

Meanwhile the hipster clothing freakout and monism (one rag was as weird as another and as raggy as well) had them reeling down at the nudist camp: they wanted their clothes back piece by piece! No they didn't. Even if they did it wouldn't have been poetic justice or any of that cause this is the world of fashion we're talkin about and it has no symmetries. It does but the symmetries involved are just stuff like geometry and boy-girl, not overall anything or other. In fact symmetry, geometry and form are a drag and it was the dopers who were the culprits who prevented their ultimate demise, those goddam psychedelic bastards!

Flag jackets showed up around ten years ago and they appeared before ski jackets, they were first because summer comes before winter and skiing is winter activitiy and boating (boat flags are the source of flag jacket flags) is strictly summer fun. Both were once for aristocrats but there were—as you'll no doubt remember—many social changes in the 1960's. Now everybody skis and ski jackets are an everywinter item while only one or two in any crowd go boating and so flag jackets have passed away as continuing wearables. But not just because they had upper middle class affinities. No it was cause there were supposed to be 26 different flags (one for every flavor of the alphabet), each with a minor reworking of the red-yellow-blue-black-white (two or three at a time) formula for square and triangle, and yet only one design out of the whole bunch was really popular (red, yellow triangles on blue). And not every apparel fancier wanted to be caught with the same covering as everybody else around his arms and torso. Jackets themselves are a tremendous drag anyway but the constancy of seasonal change is even worse. So instead of aping the Motor City's annual hoochiekoo the clothiers and haberdashers put their thinking caps on and decided it was a good idea to occasionally keep something forever if it happens to have eternal seasonal import: ski jackets and they'll be with us as long as blue jeans.

Sandals too. It's another summer item, open and breezy and you can wiggle your toes. And you can do enjoyable things like paint your toenails and wear rings on your toes. And everybody can even see it since you're not wearing shoes. And you can step in puddles and your feet get all wet. If you're still wearing them when fall comes around you can kick leaves with your toes.

Military dress never changes. Space suits haven't changed in over ten years. Cops and zoo keepers are unchanged too. But the one publicly prominent arena of life where dress has been changing radically is, of all places, among bridge and tunnel officers (toll collectors). The reason for the change is they now have women where they used to have just men. And in such areas codes of dress remain rigidly conventional, you can tell one's sex as readily by his or her clothing as by his or her genitals.

Aprons have lost their status in the kitchen as well as dining room as sloppiness has become one of the highest virtues and napkins and that whole line of paper products have been making up for inadequacies in sleight of hand with food. You can and do throw napkins away after use not so much because they're food-stained as because they're wrinkled and inexpensive. So why not paper aprons and paper clothing and in particular paper undergarments (if we're to wear those things at all anymore, and the trend seems to be against it)? That's exactly what's been happening! But for the sake of e-college-y it should all be recycled and for a lesson in that we oughta set our sights on the Bowery.

Derelict outerwear hasn't changed much over the last few decades at all, they're all still wearing sportjackets and pants. At the end of the 20's and 30's and 40's and 50's there might have been a few original double breasteds lying around waiting to get picked up and preserved by being worn. Well those old numbers have finally worn out due to use—sort of like a tire. So the wardrobe content on skid row is probably early-60's by now (give a bum a Nehru jacket sometime while you can still get your hands on one—they could disappear right before your eyes) so why not take the initiative and speed up the process, give away all your recent items that you're sick of, just dump em in the street down there and if the garbage man finds em first that's fine too, he needs some variety himself, both in what he garbages and what he keeps.

And after you've gotten rid of what you don't want you'll be wanting stuff to take its place and why should it be any harder for you to get the unpleasant job done of selecting your shit than it is for Mr. Skids? So get hep and here's how: pay some gent off the street to pick the items for you in the store while you close your eyes and then just get each thing in your own size. Or the cheaper way where the guy who picks out your clothes is your friend. And cheaper is better because it keeps the economy strong and without the economy there'd be no clothes, or food, or even shelter.

What would Katy Keane say about the latest fad in girls' underwear on guys, if she were alive would she agree that after all it's smoother and more comfortable all around and comes in many colors? And vice versa, would the fabled miss know-it-all of haute couture agree likewise that guys' underwear on girls is more convenient for reaching thru the crotch hole to masturbate in language lab in school and those crotchless panties cost so dear?

If football numbers are a key to personality—and there's every reason to believe they are—why's the only number they got on them for civilians so far the much overworked 69? For instance Tim Rossovich of the Philadelphia Eagles has never gone the oral-genital route and his number is 82. Two times four equals eight and the four was two squared to begin with. Thus there's plenty of old-fashioned squarehood in the number and it sums up his lifestyle better than 69. Also it sums up his life better than Fran Tarkenton's number 10, the symbol of decimal solidarity, hence emotional stability and also a one followed by a very big zero. And if there's anything Fran is it's one who's a very big zero! So it's no 69 for him, even off the field where he can wear whatever the fuck he wants while he's sitting with his family around the fireplace popping corn. But for some people 69 is *just perfect*, for instance the late Marilyn Monroe.

She was no square and neither were her handkerchiefs. When she blew her snout or wiped off the snot it was always into a kleenex (one of the earliest uses of paper in the boudoir) and they're *rectangular*. Well some of them begin their lives as squares but the machine folds them up and over and the final product is neater than a pin and certainly neater than a hanky itself. And if you cry into them when the going gets sad it's hanky panky when you're cranky! And if you're from Spanky & Our Gang!

And if you are you might get to be on the radio: and even today it's a real problem deciding what to wear for the radio, whether AM, FM or Pacifica. So here's a tip from the Mad Meltz: wear a radio!

# Living Theater My Eye!

If there's anything living about the Living The-ate-er I ain't seen it and I'm not alone: no one has! Cause living's as appropriate to theatre as grateful is to dead, in other words it's not! (Unless you're a raving loony.) Instead of winding up they oughta be winding down, they're looking for drama just like Connie Francis used to be "Looking for Love" and doing the looking "Where the Boys Are"! They're guilty of *dramatic chauvinism* of the worst sort and should be dealt with accordingly as *just a bunch of fuckin aesthetes like all the rest*!

But at least they're willing to listen so maybe they'll hear this plea to disband their whole show and go into hog farming. One of the things they were willing to hear was critiques of the classical stage that were not pleasant for the sensitive ear such as: CLASSICAL THEATER IS ALL PLAYED OUT and it was so loud they had to pay attention and they didn't stop there, they went on and did something about it, they started ignoring the stage. But they still used it! After all stages whether they're high or low are still flat planes and the world at large isn't flat at all. So they packed up their satchels and their makeup and props and headed down to the unflat mountains of Brazil, the smartest move they ever made but they didn't take one thing into account: sometimes even an unflat stage is gonna wanna call the shots with all those *actors* steppin on it all the time and all. And like why do you gotta have actors at all except to prove that it's *living* and aren't plants alive too as well as the whole planet anyway? Redwood trees live longer than people so they oughta play all the parts or there'll be a lotta dead corpses on Julian Beck's hands before the turn of the next century and the name'll be as outmoded as THE MODERN JAZZ QUARTET. And lots of horses are dead already so why kick a dead horse when you know that the last curtain went down on theatrical performance in 1951 or thereabouts with the last performance of *The Crucible* starring Samuel Beckett? Artificial respiration won't work either so give up, it's time for an unconditional surrender to the forces of intergalactic pumice!

# Wabbits on Babitz

If her name was Eve Babcock then it would be: tick tock on Babcock. But the Eve in question is a Babitz and there is no Adam in her life. People who don't have things often want them. If they want them real bad sometimes they buy them or even—if they are imaginative and able—*make* them. Such is the path of the artist, to make. Also they're allowed to unmake too, such as by cutting and destroying. And they're allowed to use glue, paste, etc. Sometimes that includes paper and when it comes to paper Eve's standing in line since last nite. Cause that's what she does, paper.

Not the newspaper either, altho Eve doesn't shy away from it for no good reason. It's just that newspapers are nothing but words and Eve's a picture person, maybe even a picture pervert and she pastes them all together in the manner begun more than half a century ago by the one and only famous Georges Braque of Europe. Him and Pablo used to paste stuff and it was called papier collé and shortened for the layman's convenience to collage. Collages are prestige items in the best of homes and Eve does them for just such a purpose and is well rewarded for her work. Michael Bloomfield of Chicago said, "She can boogie all nite long."

In other words: 1) she's like a bunny for guitarists and singers; 2) she realizes it's important to pursue the great god Dollar; 3) art and life mix easy (in her case).

And here's of which her artifacts consist. They consist of likenesses of the stars and flowers and pieces of linoleum. "Very good," you probably say. Wrong! Very bad because the first rule of art is looks good. Hers does not. Rules were made to be broken but not the sanctity of art. For instance: the one she did of Stevie Winwood. It's his face in grey like from the photograph she cut it out of (she didn't take it and somebody should invoke the copyright law before the statute of limitations runs out) and the background is brown linoleum and his suit is the same brown linoleum but a different portion of the same piece or maybe it's from wallpaper. Her signature graces the lower righthand corner in green.

Now the above may seem like an archaic way of dealing with things and indeed it is, it is the well oiled "critical method" handed down by the 15th century rationalists who are all gratefully dead. Maybe they're not grateful but we are or if we're not we should be. Throw that method out the window!

In its place let's substitute the modern method. First things first. Her actual works of art. Namely her cover for the second Buffalo Springfield album, her cover for Black Oak Arkansas, her John Lennon collage, her Eric Clapton collage, her Ginger Baker collage, her Rick Grech collage, the xerox called "Mona Lennon" that she sent Diane Gardiner (she's got John Lennon on the brain apparently). Next, decide which one is worst. Decide as you may but you can't, no one is worse than any other. Therefore, by logic, *all her objets d'art stink to high heaven*. Empirical verification backs this up, and that's the modern method of evaluation.

There's a method in the middle between the old one and the new one that makes some sense, and that's to ask an expert. No greater expert has ever furrowed his brow than Marcel Duchamp and so why not ask him? Because he is deceased so you can't. So why even bring him up? Because he actually appears in a photog's dream of a pitcher with Eve taken by somebody. Marcel is playing chess with her and and it's hard to tell who's winning. Could the old master have consented to be located inside the same rectangle with her if he did not respect her to the utmost? Most likely not except for one really significant matter: her works do not appear within the confines of the photo altho his do. Conclusion: he prefers (or should we say *preferred*) his own objets to hers. Also: objets trouvés are superior to objets d'art any day of the week. So if you ever trouve one of her efforts it'll be good then but in order for that they have to be lost first. And she won't lose them, she guards them with her life so there's only one recourse if you're seriously interested in the intrinsic artistic potential of her stuff. But I'm not telling it cause art should remain a mystery.

# Paper and Hard

Trees were made to bear leaves but as it's worked out they've been made to get hacked so they can put out the Sunday *New York Times* on time without looking for a paper substitute. Like plastic could be used but not yet, they haven't done it yet but they may before the century is out and done with. But they're still busy cuttin the wood and gettin it wet and mushy so they can prepare paper. The best use of paper yet invented is spitballs and the second best is cardboard and the third best is postcards with pictures of famous places. Cardboard can't be made outa books (the eighth best use of paper) and postcards can't either but spitballs can and since they're the best therefore books are okay. And when they're the hard variety they can be used to kill fruit flies that have settled on a mirror to check out their appearance.

Books such as Kathleen Freeman's *Ancilla to the Pre-Socratic Philosophers* on the Harvard University Press for $4.00. The cover is green and it's made of cloth but sometimes cloth gets thrown in with the paper brew too and cloth comes from a plant like the trees so everything is more than alright. The outside dust cover's an attractive light blue with dark blue letters with serifs. The typeface inside is mondo swell.

And who, for instance, could remain uninterested in the pre-Socratics, and our own hero Heraclitus, after reading Flambeau's *Melissus of Samos* and *Eurytus of Southern Italy*, or after being fascinated by the somewhat different picture of him presented by Maurice Hewlett in his *Heraclitus Yea and Nay*? But even if novels can give us that keen interest in the heroes of the past, we may still feel all the same, that after all the novel presents only the point of view of somebody living at a time nearly as remote from the persons he depicts as we do ourselves. His story may bear all the impress of verisimilitude, yet, after all *he* was not present at the scenes he describes; he did not look upon the beauty of Aphrodite, tremble beneath the frown of her imperious cousin Athena, nor join in the revels that marked the coming of Poseidon into his kingdom. It is for this reason that such books as these we have been mentioning are especially interesting, for they *are* written by people who took part in the scenes they describe. Fielding knew people whose ideas and manners were just those of the characters to whom he presents us, Pepys and Evelyn were actually present at the places, and really met the people of whom they speak. Above all they were people of their own age, reflecting alike its gravity and its folly, its manners and its thoughts, and so, almost more with them in their own surroundings and so enlarge our mental content and experience in a way that nothing else could do. Kathleen Freeman is such a one.

And so is Norman Lemon Peel, author of *The Power of Postivie Drinking* (Pyramid Books, New York, 128 pp., $.40). No he's actually the editor but it's a holidé reading what he's edited. Especially the page with the picture of the new taster entering the tasting room of the Ravano Wine Co. and being told by the boss "One word of caution before you take over, Beauregarde...no drinking off the job!" Then the pixker of the cat at the bar with a friendly buddy and he tells him "I'd been a 'yes' man for so long I couldn't help but agree with him when he said he was thinking of firing me." Sehr witty, is it not?

And it's only 40¢ cause the paper in the binding is not hard. And the softer the better as far as permanence goes cause who wants to keep carrying around a heavy ol' book from house to house in this mobile carefree life? When it gets *very* soft you'd think the price would go down too but not always so. S. Clay Wilson's *Bent* is priced at half a buck but that doesn't bother most readers cause he's every bit better than the vaunted Charles Dickens. Such tales as "The Cask of Amantillado," "The Gold Bug," "William Wilson" and others leave an almost uncanny impression on the mind, and few stories of the Inquisition convey such a striking picture of its terrors as "The Pit and the Pendulum." A man has come into the grip of the Inquisition in Toledo and by them is bound, full length, to a framework of wood so that he is unable to stir. Above him is a contrivance resembling a huge pendulum swinging back and forth, and gradually lengthening so as to approach nearer and nearer to him. But that's nothing compared to Wilson's "Thumb and Tongue Tales," contained in the *Bent* volume. This guy is entrapped beneath a two-by-four with a wicked spike dangling from it and meanwhile his dick is being sliced lengthwise but if he stirs he gets croaked. Either way life is not worth living but he gets it from both ends anyway after being denied any true choice, as both lingam and life are both snuffed out nearly simultaneously. But not a stone is left unturned as the Checkered Demon comes back to get someone to get a load of all the thumbs and tongues he has in his room. Yet unlike Dickens he has the wrong person brought over to see the thumbs and consequently she is dropped from the sky to a fate worse than death. And the art is an improvement on Wesselman.

# Truth Is Stranger than Poetry

It's indisputable that Ogden Nash influenced Allen Ginsberg immeasurably. They could try to measure it but the measures wouldn't be big enough to get the job done and any measures would be treasures if they could. But did you know that the engineer of verse who influenced both of them even more than that is still alive? Well she is: Melba Moses. Her name was Mose but it rhymed with hose so she made it Moses. They sampled her wares and if you haven't here's your chance:

|                     |                     |
|---------------------|---------------------|
| sure                | tuff however        |
| kentucky sutton     | that                |
| a matter of         | didn't know about it|
| longer and shorter  | younger             |

The title of that gem was "Tuff" and it sure definitely does get the point across by telling it like it is. And the rhyme and the meter (rhymes with "eat 'er") and the words and the images are flawless, due no doubt to her Piscean background. Like she always watched the *Topper* show because of its perspicacity in family matters and she left home at age 20, quite a parallel to Emily Dickinson and Nathaniel Hawthorne.

Also she was the first American poet to draw an audience for a reading of more than 2500—excepting of course colleges where admission to the reading is free. In 1953 when Ogden Nash was still a fledgling newsboy in Sarasota she came to town for an old-fashioned poetry shindig and he attended. By the time she was midway thru her first selection they were rolling in the aisles during a poem entitled "Exploratory":

exploratory
prostate surgery

Ogden unrolled himself and—according to Nate Tharz in his masterful treatise entitled "Poetry"—was a poet from that minute on. Two years later he met Allen, they hit it off real well and the rest is history.

Thereafter the Poetry Revival took place and for the first time since 1905 poetry exceeded 45,000 in annual sales. And I'm happy to report that in the calendar year 1971 sales reached a peak of 71,500. You may not know this but at the Alternate Media Conference of a short time ago Melba decided that poetry should be free so from now on sales may go down cause she's only giving it away now and encouraging others to do same and support themselves by working for the post office.

So far the move towards free poetry hasn't quite picked up that much steam however, as evidenced by the latest Internal Revenue survey. It says there were 350 poets with incomes of $23,000 or more in the April '71 returns and since the postal salary is less they must still be supporting themselves via poetry!

But things may change overnite so you gotta have heart.

# Hot Pucks

Football may be the big thing in both places but in one there's another big thing called baseball and in the other there's another real big thing by the name of hockey. Canada, being the land of the caribou and frozen eau you can cut with a knife, is where they do hockey cause it's suited that way. U.S. of A. has all the diamonds so they play ball. But if you have a TV and/or car you can see both in both places.

Go to the ticket man, tell him you wanna see hockey, pay him and you're all set. If the game's tomorrow or the next day you'll have to wait but if it's tonite wowee! The fans in the NHL enjoy seeing all 78 games. Even if your team is a loser be friendly, won't you? They could use it, particularly if they are having personal difficulties with their families. All the world's a slab of ice and these tremendous athletes appreciate your cheers more than your boos. The fans in Oakland arrive early to see the ice get dusted off and polished down or whatever they do to it. And between periods they never go to the hot dog stand or the rest room, they stay for the ice job then too. It's amazing and you wouldn't believe it. So if it's the Seals you're gonna go see be prepared to hold it in!

Which is better, baseball or hockey? It all depends on whether 3-strikes-you're-out is better or worse than penalty box. We'll leave that toughy for the thinkers and go on to the fun of the game which is real big. It's not the way they skate this way, that way, and this way again: it's the personalities galore that make this colorful game real good. But it takes 2 to tango and similarly a minimum of 2 teams are required for a hockey contest or exhibition. So what we're gonna do right now without hesitating one minute is take 2 of the best teams on the map and tell you what their players have to offer. Space and time prohibit mentioning each and every one—and so that credit be given where due—congrats to all other players on all other teams!

Take Barry Ulmer.

He met his 3rd wife at a public auction. She was the only one outbidding him for pucks. They got married that day and gave birth to a lovely little boy 7 months later. The kid was 2 months premature but that was pretty fast action even for the likes of Mr. Ulmer! He's fast on his skates and he's even faster with his stick, but who would have guessed it was his rod that had them beat by a mile! Naturally he drinks Pabst, which certainly hasn't stunted his growth in the you-know-where department! The inside dope: look for opposing players to inflict serious groin injury upon his person within the next 12 months.

The New York Rangers may have hornswaggled their name from the world famous Texas Rangers themselves but this has in no way aided their crusade in the prevention of groin harm to their super-stellar defenseman, the one and only Barny Aure. Needless to say he's off his blades for the time being, giving him time to pause and ask a number of serious questions. The specific injury involved is a *groin pull*, so who pulled it? Did he pull it himself or was somebody else in on the job? If it was the other team then Barny oughta let his teammates know and they'll surely prevent future mishaps. If it was him then he needs a stern lecture from the top brass of the Ranger organization or perhaps his personal physician or minister. Telling the team physician about it would take some balls but think it over Barny, your career and those of your teammates depend on it, particularly with the Stanley Cup always just a heartbeat away.

There's Bergman the hockey guy and Bergman the philosopher: neither one is a jewboy! The reason: the only hockey jew is some guy who retired in Philadelphia (he had a Z in his name), the only philo jew is Bob Sternfeld. Both are bald.

Giacomin, Ed. He's the opposite of Sonny Liston the late great belter. He gets scored on rarely but it's always an obviously avoidable thing. Sonny if you'll remember was just the opposite: he'd chug along boring until the one big puncheroo which you might of missed so if you couldn't see it pity the poor chin! One time Giacomin got hurt—it was not, I repeat *not*, a major injury—and in that injury his head got *jerked back*: blood was the result and it was mouth blood, not lip blood even though it dripped down his lip, but MOUTH BLOOD. Hence, an internal injury. Everybody knows internal injuries are worse than external injuries, only God knows the reason. So if he opened his mouth a bit more like ex-Ranger Gump Worsley (who has yelled

"Fuck shit piss" more than once on the hot ice in the heat of battle) it would be an *external* injury. It doesn't have to be swear words, but open your mouth more Eddy!

No one is more tenacious at puck clutching than Roy Edwards, goalies included, which Edwards is which is a good, good thing for so defensive a player. Just think what they'd do if he was a forward! His ass would be full of so many bench splinters they'd have to apply special ice packs between periods when he was standing up.

Balon is a dead ringer for Paul Butler who works for the federal govt. of the United States of America, another great team in another great league. He's got the heart of a bull or a shark and knows his team is still alive until the final gun goes off. Considering the El Foldo the Rangers are engaged in each and every season that's some bull!

Stemkowski is strong, he's got muscles on muscles. His wife is no slouch either, she has a nice pair of pectoral muscles that will turn you green with envy and which help her a great deal in her own favorite sport, modeling.

Seiling on the other hand has nary a muscle on his less that 6' frame. That includes his facial muscles and his heels. Gym work with barbells and the old chinning bar would be advisable for him. If you agree, write to the Rangers' trainer, c/o Mad. Sq. Garden, 2 Pennsylvania Plaza, NYC and maybe we'll see some action. But don't spread the word too much or other teams might know he's no bargain and not give up diddley-shit for this sludgebottom and the Rangers will be stuck. In that case such physical culture would be not advisable but *compulsory*. A little more mustard on his shot—both wrist shot and slap shot included—would mean more games in the win column and more games tied, both vital in the race for the cup and all the champagne orgies that go with it. No sacrifice is too great for one's hockey.

And speaking of champagne, Macgregor is proud to be a Canadian even though he is not French. He thanks the powers that be that Trudeau is his *president*, even though they don't call them that north of the border. A little less American TV and you'll get your facts straight Bruce!

Gilbert: if you got the choice between a blocked shot and an intercepted pass, take the pass, it doesn't fuck up your shooting percent. That is the credo he lives and plays by. Trade this creeptin! Here's a good trade: Gilbert & Rod Seiling for any good 2nd string goalie worth his salt. Gilbert is not worth his salt, Seiling isn't worth his MSG, he isn't worth his weight in orlon and he's no lightweight! Sheesus Christ!

Gordie Howe knows his angles on net like he was a protractor or something and we all know he's tuff. But why's he wear his dentures off ice? He'd be more impressive without em. I guess it's just a bizness to this oddball, like refrigeration or plumbing, and when he leaves the office for the day or nite that's that. Too bad: too many teeth in your life is never any good. Imagine if everybody went around adding teeth to their mouth: dentists would be making a fortune! They'd be the king of the hill and not hockey people, which is not to be desired. Howe's birthday is March 31, making him miss April by one scant day. April is the last month of the season except for May and March is close behind, a valuable time to celebrate your birth. And for his birthday let's hope a well-meaning fan gives him some denture cream which is actually harmful lye. Harmful to his fake teeth that is, not his own. That way there'd be the same famous gaps in his biters when you saw him on the street. He wouldn't be able to dodge autograph seekers with a full mouth disguise cause everybody'd know it was him. But come to think of it that way he'd have trouble chomping on his three squares a day, perhaps endangering his digestive tract and eventually weakening his hockey arms and legs. Keep the teeth Gordie!

Ted Irvine—you pronounce it Irvin—is an English name that's hard to pronounce for Rangers so they got him for Réal Lemieux who was easy to pronounce if you're a frenchy or had it in junior high. Wadda pick! Now they got somebody to go with Tkaczuk who's a foreigner by any standards and has two ways to pronounce his name (the obvious one and Kachook), one for each way to score a point, the goal and assist.

Mahovlich once almost came close to just about coming near breaking the season goal record, a meager 50 at the time. He never did it and he never will but I wouldn't mind if he was my father when I was a kid. That way I'd get to see all the hockey games free!

Ratelle is the face-off king bar none. He's cool, calm and collected, leaving many opponents bewitched, bothered and bewildered in his wake. Once he gets the rubber you can bet your money he'll pass it and if he gets it back he might just pass it again. But if the net is open he'll shoot and you can chalk up an entire unit for Rangers cause this cat hasn't missed since his days as a toddler. His aim is deadly accurate which points up he might be a real winner in skeet shooting or international warfare in time of crisis. It's real good that North America can depend on his stuff.

Dick Libett, in his successful 2nd full season with the Red Wings, catches a lot of hell about his penile moniker. That is when he doesn't score. So he scores if he knows what's good for him, a great asset to any team. Actually his name is Nick but it might just as well be Dick if he falls asleep on ice!

Speaking of dicks, better watch out for the taunts of Carl Brewer: he challenges your jewels with his stick and other parts of your midsection as well. Don't eat a full meal before you meet him on the blue line, that's if you fear easily. If not then it's easy sailing cause you know all he wants is you to foul him. Do it the other way round: let *him* commit the penalty!

Hooking penalties are more fun than a barrel full of peanuts. You're walking along on your skates and wham out of nowhere there's a stick or an arm grabbing you from behind and spinning you around like a fish only there are no barbs so it ain't permanent and there are no sharp points so it don't hurt. Not only do they stop the perpetrator. They make him sit out 2 minutes and you know what? You can score a goal, that's what!! And if there's a goal to be scored it might be Billy Dea who does it.

Dea plays hockey for a living and he wouldn't have it any other way. You won't be finding him on the relief rolls, but if he gets fired here comes trouble! He won't like it, so of course he would prefer being traded. He can and has scored against the Rangers, so they might welcome him with open pads in the New York area. The Rangers can either play him or bench him, if he's off ice in the hotel room at least he's not *on ice* against the home team. When he's on ice for Rangers if he's good all the more power to him. If not then they oughta fire the dork, it's that simple. It will be hard to do but can be done.

Baun is a good kicker and not even with just his foot but with skates too. The shoe doesn't hurt his great kick and neither does the blade, he's a good one. If anyone, say Ron Stewart who is an old man, has the misfortune of being in the way it could mean curtains on a great career. Injuries, bruises, pulls, rips, fractures, lacerations, abrasions all are possible. No it isn't actually Baun who's the excellent kicker, of course it's Howe. I just figured someone else deserved kudos for his hard work. Baun is good too, don't forget it.

Move up to hockey quality with Brad Park, the only one with one syllable in each name, which helps him save his strength for torrid play. His one-syllable talents abound: check, goal, stick, shoot, puck, pass, skate but also the assist and handling. But the one thing they pay him for is check. A check for his checks. Checks don't mean dirty play when it's Brad Park who's throwing them. With him it's position, poise and politeness. That's right, he'll often apologize to a fallen opponent for pain inflicted but that doesn't mean he's averse to fighting. No sir but don't count him out for the Lady Byng which will sure look good on his shelf. Alex Delvecchio has it now so watch out Alex, here comes Brad!

On ice Karlander has the same smarts that enabled him to complete a college education at Michigan Tech. And can he ever deflect! Sometimes it's to his advantage and sometimes it's not but it's always worth watching.

Roger Crozier's forte is not just acrobatics but *crouching*. When someone scores the hat trick on him he's in perfect position to pick up all the hats and bring them home. But instead he leaves them for the officials so they can be reclaimed at the lost and found, he's a swell guy and as sportsmanlike as heck!

Dale Rolfe: forward or defenseman? Looks (he's 6′4″) would dictate the former, play would dictate the latter, skating talent would align him with the former, puck stamina with the latter, his looping and intercepting make him a dead ringer for the former. That's what they call versatility in any man's book but it shows its head as ambiguity, an important prerequisite for any exciting player! He carries not just a puck, stick and knee pads but also the number 18. When he tangles with Tkaczuk those 18's can really let the feathers fly!

Jim Neilson may not be the only Indian in big league hockey but his warpath antics are sure hard to beat! And there ain't nobody—I don't care if you're Rocket Richard himself—as well versed in preventing excessive icing in a tight game. Jim doesn't *like* skating down ice just to make contact with the puck so they can bring it back and start all over again, that's not his meat, he likes heads-on rough-and-ready. So you better not ice it when he's around, he'll scalp you!

The corners of the rink aren't exactly what you call corners strictly speaking. After all they're round as you can get, any rounder and who knows what they'd call them but don't tell Fairbairn he doesn't do much in the corners. He'll first call you a liar, next he'll challenge you to prove it, he'll dare you and double dare you to try him out next time you're both on the frozen surface together. If you're Jack Egers that would be the very next practice. If you're playing against Bill in practice he'll eventually be in one of those "corners" with you and the puck and who will win? Bill of course. He'll dazzle you with finesse and perseverance while you show nothing in return. But say you're on the same side during practice, then there would be no decisive way of proving anything once and for all so it might go unresolved forever!

Bruce Gamble is a lousy goalie. But he covers it up by playing good enough to pass for not half bad. He looks, especially around the face, like a fat Gil Hodges with sideburns and no teeth. He's real easy to beat if you score on him. Score the tie goal and then all you have to do is score the go-ahead goal. Once in a while his glove save is no good. Once in a while his stick save is no good. Once in a while both. He's not as good as Johnny Bower. He's not as good as César Maniago. He's not as good as Rogatien Vachon. He can get faked out real easy. He's not as good as Desjardins. He's not as good as DeJordy. His name is Bruce Gamble. Caught on his way off the ice the other day he said "I'm a good goalie." But he's not. Nor is he a Ranger or Red Wing. But he might be some day! A bad goalie might not be a bad idea, it's just like the draw play or a broken-legged pinch runner only sneakier. That way you can't blame the team for losing, only the dunce in the net. He'll have nightmares, ulcers and a bad back but if you tell the rest of your men it's his fault they'll sleep easy and win a few games themselves. Sleep and rest hold the key.

How's this for a trade: Kurtenbach for Shack, their names

rhyme. In fact it would be good bizness to require rhyme trades and rhyme trades only. Don Awrey from Boston to Toronto for Jim Dorey. Brad Park for Bob Clarke. Savard and Richard for Picard. And a number of 3-team trades. Mahovlich gives up his Red Wing uniform for a King hockey suit, Ravlich throws away his L.A. King outfit for a Pittsburgh Penguin sweatshirt, Woytowich heads on over to Detroit to complete the deal. And a 4-teamer: Gray from the Blues to the North Stars, O'Shea from the North Stars to the Red Wings, Dea from those guys to the Black Hawks, McKay over to St. Louis. Tony Esposito rhymes with Phil Esposito so that's an easily consummated one-for-one deal. It doesn't rhyme perfectly but it's good enough when you wheel and deal Bobby Sheehan for Gerry Ehman. Ron Ellis for Ron Harris is a real showstopper. Same for Tkaczuk and the late Sawchuk for Miszuk. Dick Cherry for Ross Lonsberry. Marotte for Marcotte. Harry Howell for Wally McDowell, who isn't in the bigtime but might be some day soon. Last but by no means least, Jean Ratelle for Doug Favell. But of course such speculation is fanciful. If you were the commissioner himself you couldn't do it. But if you were all 14 owners you could. That's sure the kind of thing any gent in the chips with boring times ahead should consider: buy all the teams! If they don't let you, pay somebody else to buy it for you! It may take longer but it will be worth the wait. Sooner or later you can do what you want! And people and fans alike will gasp at your actions! Sounds good and it's true.

# Some Things Are Better Left Unsorted

I saw an ad for some new snuff called Cökesnuff and figgered it was either jesus fuckin great or white like that other white stuff or at least a new one so it's worth tryin out. So I sent in my two bucks in cash for the sampler and what I got back was the biggest surprise in all the days of my life, TWICE the amount of snuff I expected and a letter addressed personally to yours truly:

> Hi Richard
> You must be the same cat snuffing in the April Rags.
> I'd like to hear your comments about Cökesnuff.
> Rap with me sometime—215-732-6300
> 215-Ch8-9408
> Call collect
>> Thanks
>> *Leslie Tobin*

First I tried the patchouli flavor Cökesnuff and just the sight of the tobac clued me in as to why there's that umlaut on the Coke, it's brown not white. A quick cursory snort and where was the flavor? One more and *what* was the flavor? Menthol maybe but not much patchouli but there was a decent sneeze.

Cherry next and then I knew what the score was. This was just another run-of-the-mill pseudo-flavored American-made brown dunger like Garrett and all the rest even though it was made in England. There's all these others like Highland Mills and they're all worthless even as a last resort in a town where there's nothin else. Cherry Cökesnuff's no exception and neither is the flavor: none. Well there's the flavor of the tobacco with a little hint of polyethylene (hey they could have airplane glue flavor but they don't) and it's not even a sneezer.

Jasmine! Yeah sure it's jasmine, my ass it's jasmine, some perfumes have jasmine and this one's plenty perfume-y but no jasmine in sight. Bad aftertaste too so it's on to strawberry right fuckin away!

That's what they call it but if it's strawberry I'll eat the tin, it's more like a carrot but maybe it's just a cross between the jasmine and the cherry and it smells just like a model of the U.S.S. F.D.R. without the glue so patchouli's lookin better and better.

Patchouli. Not bad. Mighty fine. Same kind of tickle but sneezing's out this time cause of the rough time caused by the other stuff to the nasals which means it's as good a time as any to check out the others one more time.

Cherry. If you *really* work on it and think it over it's kinda like cherry pie cherries already in the pie and cooked but it's too hidden to do much good. But there's some promise.

Strawberry again! Kiss the shit goodbye, it's not even rhubarb!

Jasmine tastes like strawberry *and* there's a sneeze so maybe somebody at the snuff plant mixed up the labels (could be).

Patchouli's mild and unobjectionable and even the tobacco taste is out of the picture so it's the best to offer somebody if you don't wanna ruin his day. But it's not what a good snuff should be, a pair of shades for your nose. If it is then it's pretty clear lenses so I guess I'll just file my report to Leslie Tobin right now:

Les, your snuff is—to put it mildly—a rip-off of all honest hardworking snuffers with two bucks to kill on a new hit. As with all snuff tasters I went thru the ordeal of clearing out my passages with Dristan and a lotta water's gonna go under my bridge before I get fooled again. I did not call you collect because I would not soil my hands on the telephone just for your benefit. If you were an elephant I would stick your entire stash up your trunk. Never in my life have I, you can betcha life you vermin.

> Fuck you, you criminal,
> *R. Meltzer*

But since the Cökesnuff people were so kind to send me double the amount ordered Leslie (male or female?) deserves a break:

Dear Leslie,

Thank you very much. Patchouli tastes best, jasmine is second, cherry is third, strawberry is fourth, in that order. Made in England is it? Well keep up the imports!

> Best of luck,
> *R. Meltzer*

# Smokem

They don't give bubble gum cigars for births and they don't give them when they're kids either. Kids keep their bubble gum cigars and use them for their own personal use. Sometimes a bubble gum cigar will be given *to* a kid by an adult or the rich kid on the block and sometimes they're occasionally given out at parties. But kids never give them to mother and daddy as a present because that would be extremely rude because adults do not blow bubbles even if they do chew gum. Grownups like the real thing and they should give the real thing too, they should give their *kids* the real thing especially. In order to teach them proper behavior they should give them real cigars and matches to light them. Is matches the reason kids are forbidden to smoke except behind the barn? This question is still the subject of controversy.

But once the cigar's lit and the match is extinguished the only fire is in a small area at the end of the cigar. But not if it's one of those fine stogies from the Cherokee Trading Post in Budd Lake, N.J. Those are the real fat ones and don't let the price tag fool you into thinking they're crud just cause they're only 49¢ for two inches in diameter and a foot and a half long. No, no, a thousand times no: don't let the tag fool you but they're still fire hazards and you can burn a hole in a person's face and shirt with em.

And you can inhale the smoke and it's smooooooth as silk, smooooooth as satin, and smooooooooth as butterscotch pudding. Not at all like burning meat but there *is* a hint of meat in it. Somehow without oxidizing meat the taste of meat still comes out, that is with oxidizing something other than meat the taste of meat comes out and it isn't even the taste of burned meat. Tastes like those burning punks too, the ones they used to burn before they had incense back in the early 50's in the summertime. From Budd Lake and there's some mighty good swimming there but don't swim or you'll extinguish your cigar and don't take your seegar there in winter or you'll fall thru the ice and lose it to the cold dark water. Then it can't be retrieved until the following spring so you'll have to buy a new one at the Trading Post. Buy several!

(Note: Cigar smokers seldom notice their own cigar breath odor because the air they breathe passes out along the lower nasal cavities, whereas the nerve endings for the sense of smell are in the upper part. In order to prevent embarrassment the ancient Indian method should be employed of chewing on a piece of redwood bark, not available from the Cherokee Trading Post so you have to send away for it because the CTP is INAUTHENTIC.)

# Guilt Moistens the Door

There are more beards than there were four years ago and there are also less. More because more people have them and less because some people have cut them off. Visual shit aside, there's just no way of getting around that goddam itch so some guys have cut them off and at least one bearded lady too. Kissing has gained in the process too, you ever kiss somebody with a beard (unless it's soft and that's rare)?

One of the good things about a beard is you save calories when you eat porridge out of a feedbag cause some of it gets caught in your beard so you don't eat the whole thing and you lose some weight. If you're a pro star on a weight program that's no good but pros don't eat porridge anyway, they eat steak and stew and Team Flakes. Team Flakes is good because it has the same nutritional value as a shot of whiskey but when you eat a shot of scotch you can't get your beard in it but you can in a bowl of Team Flakes.

But Team Flakes can jam a razor so shavers always wash their beard first if they value their blades. And blades is plural cause there's more than one variety, electric and acoustic. And both can be used in tandem and often are. First you shave the front of the face with the electric. Then all that's left is under the chin and on the neck if it goes down that far. So the acoustic gets called into action there because it does a better job than the electric cause electric's no good for concavities like under the chin, 's the way it goes!

'S also the case that Edge IS NOT WHAT IT SAYS IT IS for under the chin (and over the chin neither). It says it lubricates the face so you don't get cut but you do if you use inferior blades (Schick is *inferior*, brother). Superior blades are Wilkinson bonded blades and superior cream is Rise Lime which never fails and makes it a joy to shave, even for hippie dippie zippies.

And speaking of lime and speaking of rise Dick Higgins ain't much of a cook (he's got a beard so it figures: natch). He doesn't know his lime cause he doesn't shave with it so when he was making poori recently—that's that Indian bread that rises like a blowfish—he used lime water from a lime when he was supposed to use lime water as in limestone (a base rather than an acid). So it came out sour (!) and it didn't even rise! Poor Dick!

And speaking of cutting hairs there oughta be a law. Like if some guy (this only applies to the male gender for obvious reasons) with lots of hair on his head and/or face does something nasty and mean he should be strapped down and given a blindfold if he wants one. No he shouldn't even get the blindfold, he should get a mirror! So he'd have to watch as they cut if off to LAME PEOPLE'S LENGTH cause lame is what he be. A recent offender in this regard is King Street Smith. It was a party and beer was in the refrigerator at his house and a guest went looking for beer and there was none left and he noticed a bottle of champagne and—assuming it to be not off limits—opened it to share with other festive partiers. King Street got so furious he said "That's a *bummer*, what gave *you* the right to open it?" to which the beaten person replied "I brought a bottle of Gordon's gin and so I thought somebody else brought the champagne" to which Mr. Smith impolitely spit "What kind of fool are you to think a *magnum of champagne* could be equated with the swill you brought?" So many people were harmed by Smith's diatribe against the humble drinkers of the party that his hash and donation of the apartment for the party in no way excused the anti-populist hideousness of his personality. Therefore his hair should be cut right the fuck off so he has NO CAMOUFLAGE to hide behind cause he doesn't deserve it!

# Mill Valley Taters

If you don't like the urbs and you don't like the wilderness then all that's left is the suburbs. Which can sure be a hardship if that's where you dropped out of to begin with. And suburbs is the latest (circa two-three years up to today) HIPPIE EXPERIMENT IN LIFE-STYLE and the foremost locale for this latest bout of *middle class jaundice* is the much benigned Mill Valley where one of the favorite pastimes is parties. But parties have always been prevalent all over environing Marin and ditto for families. There were families six years ago (even if they were loosely defined then to include only *blood* and *genes* and *wedding bands*) and they had parties and there are families now and they have parties and friends get invited too just as then.

A typical then: Guests arriving on the nether shores of Susan's mother's green and gold bug-chase night light, festive and ominously flatulent. Inside, a perturbated image of a rotten fleur-de-lis throughout the patterned wallpaper. Elihu and Pam doing a turbulent merengue to a 69¢ Tito Puente 33-1/3er in the dead center of the vast saline living room while Rosie makes a beeline for Harmon telling stories of the checker academy where he once taught Jonas Salk. Ned snoring and occasionally licking his lips over by the blind indoor lemon tree just below Tab's perfect attendance trophy. Psoriasis and dandruff running rampant on the face and scalp of Macdougal kneeling behind Hammy's ocarina redemption coupon embossed by a genuine Vienna master. Not quite audible croaks from the bullfrog Junior brought back from camp only to prefer it to peas and creamed spinach. Grapeshot being alluded to in implicit charades everywhere. Russ Tamblyn, Tamburlaine and Tamerlane being overly confused by Jill who has recently been under the knife with that cystic ovary in Venezuela. Ronald from around the corner the one friend too many trying vainly to discuss his success with the county's only tank-car full of black widow spiders. Brad on the lumpy cushion unhappy about Neville's denture odor but glad to see June with the pretty unobtrusive dimple. Bernice and Winnie smiling like babes at the discovery of each other's vaccination marks and drinking Granny Goose pink lemonade in the plush corner behind the chewed-up but still pompous couch with trumpet-and-trombone upholstery. Anita manifesting Gumby collection superiority with her 745 Pokies knee-deep in the not very emblematic static-free puce-colored carpet. Josh and his Beatle-length long blonde hair comparing and contrasting gang bangs and gang planks for Jeanne between nibbles on the ever-so-tasty lobster salad just arrived from the caterers. Bruno in the vanguard complaining vehemently about the creeping advance of cigarette smoke in his nook much to the dismay of Frank with his croquet mallet and Gertrude underneath the phosphorescent eye makeup with the cumquat bowl in her dishpan hand. Maxine really wanting to see Edmond's brand-new four-poster bed after seeing his new muscles. Jill cautiously testing her role as star of the sculpture three-quarters of the way between the ambiguous carrot smell location and the helium-filled blimp posited tentatively by a forgotten donor. Irene gawking from behind her bourbon and water and fumbling nervously with an earlobe. Senile Bascombe chewing blissfully on a magnet. Hilda wondering about carp. Lily having to go to the bathroom where Edmond's tongue is stimulating the clitoris of hefty Maxine. Buzzy telling little Sid that no it isn't Salt Lake City in the background of the Cesare da Sesto print hanging near the almost velour-like fireplace buttress....

That was then. Now it's entirely different like the party Archie Berg of Oink Records had for his 44th (57th?) birthday. First of all the cats and dogs were all locked in the same bedroom that had the only available bathroom in the house. Everybody was over 40 or under 30 and dope and cuss words filled the air. Even Archie's two teen offspring were allowed to attend and enjoy the festivities. Archie sat on his ass and opened the presents and the gang on hand sat around him in a semicircle applauding uncontrollably as a new sweater was unwrapped. Before that was avocado mousse and chicken tetrazzini from somewhere in Mill Valley and after that was coffee and cake. The cake was by Celesta Portman and there were two pigs on it with oink balloons above their snouts and Neil Likstone was there so the party was a flop. Also: all wine and coffee spills were wiped out immediately by the Berg daughter's efficiency with paper towels, stains in the rug were forbidden.

That was now but what kind of parties will tomorrow bring to Mill?

# F**k Xmas

Halloween parties are better than Xmas parties yet there is a relationship between the 2 holidays. Used to be when they pushed Xmas they waited until after Thanksgiving, all those Thanksgiving parades ended with Santa Claus in his sleigh (except one year in the Macy's Parade they had this guy who was supposed to be Santa's *helper* rather than the frostbitten septuagenarian himself) and the week after that Xmas was on the way in all the stores from coast to coast. Now they're starting the whole promotion job *before Halloween* and who are they kidding? They trying to cheapen Halloween or something? Those fuckers!

Xmas itself was never much of a holiday once the yule log got outlawed in Boston so it was a worthwhile treat when they started creating a whole new holiday known as Commercial Xmas, one of the best events on the entire calendar. Commercial Xmas was always a shot of adrenalin for both the better-to-give-than-receive platoon and all the suckers who had to receive all that shit too. Nobody gives presents anymore except for parents and there just ain't many of those left. So if it was just a non-present Commercial Xmas every year it would be the Capitalist Rip-Off's greatest gift to man and a Xian gesture of more than token value. But alas that ain't the story: this pre-Halloween thing has fucked it up immeasurably and it's all played out before 750 leaves have fallen and Frosty the Snowman is just a snowcloud's dream. So let's put an end to this Xmas bullstuff and Mr. X with it! He never belonged in it and he's had no business making a comeback and so if he loses his birthday as a holiday it'll be like Taiwan out of the U.N. so sign the petition to make it possible now!

In its place let's have PRESENTS FOR HALLOWEEN and there's already a more than adequate system for handling all the advance orders for this eventuality: Trick or Treat! But there's already some danger lurking on the horizon which threatens to cut down on the immense spirituality of this awesome *celebration of the fall*: cerebral palsy or muscular dystrophy or one of them is beginning to compete with UNICEF for the Halloween booty. *This must be stopped* if All Hallow's Eve is to survive as we now know it. Unless! Unless! Unless they just get wise and actually send all those crippled retard palsied sonsofbastards out trick or treating for themselves! It would be a real shot in the arm and the greatest thing for Halloween since the loup-garou!

# Toys for the Throne

There's this plastic robot without a face and then you feed a smaller plastic robot with a face into it and it ends up inside the bigger one and it becomes the face. But it's not really the face, it's actually the brain! It's the brain of the original big one because it's inside and faces are on the surface and the surface is still clear transparent plastic so in effect it never gets a face. So the little one is the brain and it can order the big one around and one of the orders it can give is to have the big one pick up two other small ones one in each hand. They get picked up with the robot's arms way out and if you've ever tried to lift stuff with your arms way out and perpendicular to your body you know it's not easy so this is some strong robot!

Webster's Seventh New Collegiate Dictionary defines toy as 1 *obs* a: amorous dalliance: FLIRTING b: PASTIME, SPORT; also: a sportive or amusing act: ANTIC 2 a: something paltry or trifling b: a literary or musical trifle or diversion c: TRINKET, BAUBLE 3: something for a child to play with, right that's the one, that's the definition that applies, the one about *kids*. It's the kids who have to get stuck with the fuckin toys and why them? Why do kids have to play with King Ding? That's the name of the robot, KING DING! Poor fuckin kids, poor, poor fuckin kids.

*But* if they have the imagination they can turn their toys into tools which is what robots are supposed to be to begin with, they're supposed to serve man and not just entertain him. And robots that need you to stick their brains in are no damn good unless they're intended that way to be educational. They can teach a tot that nothing does shit without a brain. But they don't, they just entertain like Frank Sinatra when they should be serving mankind and kidkind as well. So here's what a child can do with his King Ding: break it. That way it'll have to get repaired and there'll be new jobs for the unemployed. If the unemployeds don't have the skill then they'll have to go to school and that way even more people get jobs and their familes don't starve and guess what: THEN THEY'LL BE ABLE TO BUY THEIR KIDS KING DINGS TOO!

# Radio Roundup

There are only four stations still on the air that don't have a D in them. One of the quartet, Chapel Hill's WSSW, also happens to be America's oldest licensed outpost of Marconi's Folly and it features progressive programming from 6 to 9 PM with jolly deejay Lar Tusbin—he's a howl. The others are KNRR (Poland, Arizona), KUNG (Beverly Hills, Oregon) and WPAL (Craig, New Hampshire), all of them so hideous in their backward ways they do not merit a mention. KUNG for instance functions only between the hours of 6:30 and 9:45 AM for clock radio purposes only. WPAL for instance presents a weekly opera series called "Voices en Sacrae" and if the opera runs over one hour in length they cut it off and not just over the air—they own the opera so they cut it at the source!

It's common knowledge by now that Detroit Annie was perhaps the most successful new jock in the modern era and yet she was given the axe by Lamebrains Incorporated, better known as WPLJ. They may carry on and say it's white port lemon juice but it's more like walled potty loose jowls and they didn't like the way Annie took liberties with her liberty and justice for all, those fuckin peabrains! Those fuckin peabrains!

*11:05-12 Noon, WNDT: Series Four* with Ben Givaudan and guests Anne Perret and Rodrigo de Zayas. But one Anne's not gonna make up for the loss of another.

AM, FM, AM, PM but what the doggone dickens is worth tuning in except the time and temperature? R&R? Nope, R&B? A thousand times noze. Cause they're even worse than on record cause you gotta *wait* for what you wanna hear and who's got the time? You can't pick the cuts you want unless you call in and that won't do you no good unless you're Mr. Big, the only thing better than concerts about it is your finger on the volume knob. Pray for static! Get a horse! The only thing good about the wireless these days is when it's attached to a car or Joe Franklin or Zacherle or if you're lonely and want something to talk to you or if you wanna dance in the streets and you don't know how to hum or whistle or play an instrument or sing aloud. But you can take care of that with one of those portable record victrola things (and did you know that when radio first came out with broadcasts the sales of records went way down real quick and sheet music too and now sheet music is gone except for sheet musicians and records and radios are still around as archaic as ever and wait til they say the same thing later on about the picture-phone).

News broadcasts hourly on the hour: WQXD, WVND, WNED, WOD, WDFM, WMDA, WNDN, WHD, WDDD, WDER, WSDX, WTYD. Five minutes to the hour: WABD (also five minutes to the half-hour), WNMD, WPID, WRFD. Fifteen minutes past the hour: WUDP, 8:15 AM-11:15 PM. On the half-hour: WPAD, WWDJ, WNED, WLID, WWRD, WNBD, WEDD, WDAI, 6:30 only. Continuous news: WIND, WDBS. That's a wholelotof stations and an equally large number of freakquencies and that's the only good thing about radio: there's so many stations you won't be satisfied with just one and there's nobody stopping you from having all of them!

Here's the best thing to do with radio. Pull out the plug. Slice away the insulation in one spot. Make sure the two wires are touching. When the radio enthusiast plugs it back in it shorts out! Lots of sparks!

Alex Bennett once allowed David Walley on his show. If that don't beat all! Television's smarter so it's never been hoodwinked by the crumb. If you're listening to the radio right now *turn it off*, turn it the fuck OFF!

# Sing It, Tlingit

Richard Dick's his name and this guy's the real McCoy, an authentic Alaska Tlingit, Eagle clan. History says he's the first of his people to compose, sing in both English and Tlingit, and accompany himself on electric guitar. Some people have done one or the other but nobody but Mr. Dick has ever done the whole thing. But there's no real movement afoot to keep his songs as Tlingitistic as poss. So as a result he's made his first alb effort, *Alta Marie*, a contempo ballad tribute to the little woman who shares his life, not to mention his bed and board. It seems all that traditionalism he's put up with in the famed and famous Days of '98 Show (he's done his act before an estimated 300,000 in 10 years) has decided him against continuing it on vinyl. But it still has a way of asserting itself by showing thru, thru and thru.

The material on this disc is divided between the mere love song pap of "Alta Marie" (that's his wife), "Don't You Know," "You Know I Love You" and "Don't Ever Leave Me," and the geographic missivehood for tourists of "Come Home to Skagway Valley" and "In the Valley of the Wind." Skag's supposed to mean wind in Tlingit or Alaskan or something, or maybe it's the whole word Skagway that means wind. That's just the kind of bilingual gimmickry that makes lyric writing as easy as pie, it's all naive enough so that skag doesn't even mean skag, at least there's no cross-linguistic double entendre!

And the same kind of half-assedhood pervades the way he sings his tales d'amour. Like the way when an outsider is describing a singer of an alien persuasion by saying the guy sings thru his nose, Richie doesn't exactly do that but it's in the same neck of the tundra. But it's his unbridled *seriousness* which gives his performance that splendid balance of poignancy (sob) and laughingstockhood (ho ho ho). Plus he's genuinely untarnished by musical training, his picking is minimal, nothing obtrusive or fancy or well-conceived, just an occasional chord that somebody must've shown him somewhere along the line. The whole effect is like where you see these movies of the thirties where there's a pack of Okies singin and pickin on the side of the road but the guys they hired to play the Okies are slicker than shit and they have trouble faking being unprofessional and downhome. But with Dick Dick it's an attempt from the unprofessional side of the fence at their sort of professional pseudo-unprofessionalism that makes him so groove-y, particularly since the attempt is a failure.

You can order this one from either of two addresses (no it's not in any store down the block unless you live on the right block): Richard Dick, P.O. Box 226, Skagway, Alaska 99840; Richard Dick, 2705 Mission, Fort Worth, Texas 76109 (that's where his mate's originally from so there must be some business contact and she's a divorcee so that could explain it).

# A Thousand Miles Behind

After Miles did *Kind of Blue* his albums got kind of dull. By the time he got to *Seven Steps to Heaven* (introducing Tony Williams who in all fairness DID NOT HELP ELEVATE THE SESSION) it was listless flypaper galore and his worst cover up to that point including his covers on Prestige. But at least he still had his makeout albums to draw respect from, people were still making out to *Kind of Blue* and *Someday My Prince Will Come* (with his wife on the cover as the unprecedented first black model for an album not her own on a white label) and *'Round About Midnight*. And speaking of Round Midnite they used to try to make sense out of Monk (the mock-sympathetic writers did) by saying he was "cool" as in *Birth of the Cool* which Miles had perpetrated upon the world (a move similar to the birth of the Moody Blues or, better yet, CSNY). Yeah, Miles was responible for slowing down the inevitability of the whole thing wrought by Bird and in fact devastating its commercial possibilities FOREVER. It's his fault and no one else's. Bird and Diz and all that sort of shit was selling like hotcakes in the conceptual market and then Miles came along and made the Cool Jerk and the Pacific Perversion possible: Gerry Mulligan, Jack Sheldon, Shelly Manne, Shorty Rogers, that guitar player who used to be on Steve Allen (Barney Kessel), Steve Allen, etc. He fucked up the whole show and gave bebop a bad (good) name and it took Ray Charles by way of Cannonball Adderly to straighten things out but how much could they get straightened anymore, it was too late (and probably the wrong kind of straightening anyway: Miles had blown the whistle on both the formal and ethnic dimensions of jazz and all that was ushered back in by commercially viable cats like Cannonball was ethnicity). Too late for Ornette to make it, too late even for Sonny Rollins to do anything but retire so's he could play what he wanted on top of the Manhattan Bridge. Too late for Monk too but then he got lucky ten years after the fact by getting his mug on the cover of *Time* (he was supposed to have been on the week the first Kennedy got offed but it got delayed six months or whatever) while Columbia was picking him up and adding him to the stable held down then by not much more than Miles. These days these pricks at Columbia are pissed off because Monk doesn't wanna do another studio album cause he's not writing any new songs and the only reason he ever had for doing an album was to commit all his songs to wax. So Columbia's giving him the bum's rush.

And speaking of makeout music, Bill Evans was on *Kind of Blue* and now he's on Columbia too (Ramsey Lewis soon to follow in an uptempo vein). There's a story that Miles once tried to get something off a certain hip miss a long time ago (he might have forgotten) in St. Louis or someplace like that, he invited her up to his room but she said no. And what company do you think she works for now? Columbia (of course).

Well anyway Miles finally decided to do something to improve his prestige which had waned after years of being token jazzbo for this same company as makeout music's makeout musician— Johnny Mathis—and so he got himself a new band that would be funky and loaded with heavy bass riffs and even have an *electric* bass and say something to THE KIDS (the kids need jazz mixed with their rock sez Joe Klee). He figured he had to atone for fucking up the progress of jazz (he didn't *prevent* Ornette or Albert Ayler but he did keep some sawbucks out of these gentlemen's pockets) or maybe he just realized his music had gone limp so he hepped up what he was doing and it came out *In a Silent Way/Bitches Brew* et al featuring the equally nouveau hepped up Tony Williams crowd (plus of course Mr. Muzak himself the everpopular John McLaughlin). Woody Herman didn't sell out the Fillmore East but then neither did Miles (Columbia's own Laura Nyro—one of Miles' avowed favorites—headed the bill so it was her they were buying) but at least they started buying his records again now that going all the way had supplanted making out.

But there's no reason to utterly condemn the man without a fair trial which he can answer to on his own terms. We don't want this to be another GOBI (goddam ox bow incident) do we? Okay so let's slip back to the beginning when he was the son of a dentist and white kids used to bother him so he went back home to Pop Davis and the fast-thinking DDS went for his rifle. It was okay to help out little Miles by fending off racist shit but then when Charlie Parker hit town he was not so helpful to his pride-and-joy. It was the 1940's and junior was only 17 and he jammed with Bird and Bird told him Miles come with me. He was a regular Shuggie Otis but dad wasn't Johnny so he said no you must finish high school first, it was his senior year. So the senior Mr. Davis had something to do with delaying the wheels of fate but it didn't take long before the kid was Bird's trumpet man taking the world by storm. Nice stuff he was playing in those days, like neither he nor Dizzy was a Don Cherry but at least they didn't blow bad stuff.

Bad stuff was blown later on by one of Miles' numerous sidemen by the name of Hank Mobley. Hank's visible on one of those live albums with a bad cover (actually it's worse than *Seven Steps to Heaven* in that regard), *Carnegie Hall*? Anyway Hank screeched and honked and it wasn't cause he was Archie Shepp in disguise or a messenger of things to come, it was cause he was having a heap of reed trouble and the only solution was silence. Coltrane didn't play any bad stuff with Miles but—once again—it was more or less in the makeout vein all the way, just compare it to what he was laying down with Monk at about the same period and you'll see. Now today you got a man who was once about the most retrogressively lame avant-garde tenor man in the business, Pharoah Sanders. Now you're gonna say he's the cat's pajamas now and maybe that's so but all he is is a self-conscious Hank Mobley with a different approach to vibrato and a little more control. That's all but he's good sometimes. And then there's Trane's *A Love Supreme* which all the lovers of the NOW SOUND swear by and all it is is precursor to the Vanilla Fudge, Coltrane's worst and it's a good thing he's dead or I'd say it worse than that.

Meanwhile on the other front jazz has been forced into overclassicality just to survive, Ornette's had to go for grants and he signed with Columbia himself on the understanding that they'd be supplying him with an 80-piece orchestra but something was rotten in Denmark (where he once played and they ate him up there). And the whole frustrated artist riff has forced a whole lot of guys into introverted formal convolutions (and I won't even mention smack) worthy of some label's classical division but there ain't too many classical divisions left (Columbia's has Moondog). Then there's even the business about how come there ain't so many black stars on Columbia and particularly no R & B, it's cause R & B calls for payola and Columbia's all tied up with the CBS communications network so they'd lose their FCC whosis if they ever got implicated (other companies don't have to worry about that cause they just press records), Jehosaphat!

Meanwhile back to Miles, he doesn't mind Al Aronowitz!

But come on guys, let's not make a scapegoat out of Miles, leave poor Miles alone, you can't blame it all on just him and he's miles ahead of Johah Jones. Okay Miles, I exonerate you! Completely!

# Best Hair in Music

Waylon Jennings can never have the greatest country song of all time because that honor already belongs to Ferlin Husky's "Gone." But that's just because music happens to be alive and hair isn't except for the roots so hair's a shade of a difference and Waylon's got it. And does he ever have it! Merely the best toppage in a tune-related field. And since tunes include Elvis that means Waylon wins going away cause Elvis was never as good above the eyebrows and behind the ears as Waylon.

And in front of the ears too. If you examine the sideburns in early Elvis fotos it's clear they weren't unusual by today's standards and they weren't even extraordinary. They weren't even long, they didn't even reach the bottom of the ears in the lobe region, they were short. And they weren't bushy but sideburns shouldn't be bushy and Waylon's aren't either. Waylon's aren't too long either and they don't come to a point like Elvis' do today (ugly aren't they?) and Elvis' stuff on top wasn't so hot then either. Once in a while it was even skimpy like on Whit Bissell and the center of gravity was fucked, it wasn't even as good as Nick Adams. Let's face it, Elvis is lucky he wasn't a big star *today* or he'd be laughed out of the guitarists' union!

And he wasn't even a greaser! He wasn't, he was a redneck and here's the difference. Necks get red if they're exposed to the sun but if hair is long it covers the neck or if there's a tall collar. Tall collars were out then and it's only now that Elvis wears jump suits with high collars. But there's another way to avoid the redness and that's suntan oil. Being basically a grease it has the same base as hair grease and so Waylon is more of a greaser for the reason of more grease, much more grease in fact. Johnny Cash uses less grease but he does use grooming and he grooms it down over the back of his neck and you can only see the front. But you can't see it that well because his shirt is black. So is he a greaser or a redneck? Well he's not a greaser cause there's not enough grease so he could be a redneck but maybe not. Who knows, do you?

# Surefire Methods for Lunkers

In a recent issue of the outdoorsman's bible *Field & Stream* there's a fine article on catching walleye by Bob Bottomley. Fine, fine, fine in fact and it's been a big help to me with my angling so I'm passing it on to you:

"In Wisconsin many walleye fishermen minnows. Yet my best avoid using big June, September, and catches in May, taken big chubs, October have been long. Not many bait up to seven inches chubs, because dealers handle red-tail hard to keep alive these minnows are different story when for long. But it's a bait. When a chub you use them for the upper and lower is hooked through hook, he seems to last a lip with a light at least until some walleye long time—or gulps him.

"We caught all the in 22 feet of water. Hooked through the once sliding bell take the minnow swivel three feet the sinker way down. This is Lindy rig in the developed by the Minnesota our most our most popular rough day a heavier to get the minnow fish on big chubs. The chubs were mouth, and a half-sinker was used to the bottom. A above the hook prevented from sliding all the commonly called the Midwest. It was Lindy brothers in northern and has become one fishing rigs. On a sinker can be used down.

"Dozen chubs and hours. In that time that weighed five Del landed the a 10-pound two caught one that we caught three. Used them up in two we caught 18 walleyes pounds or more apiece whopper for a day, ounces, and Mark weighed 9-1/2 pounds.

"We sometimes use artificial lures, to get big fish. We but we never seem fall and early spring. Use jigs in the late often we took a crawler on the jig. We also have fairly minnow or a night good success on vibrations, but we that send out sound silver and orange plugs seldom get fish so I'm a believer. In minnows of over three pounds."

You get the picture but if you don't you well might ask *why don't these these angler-philes speak English for cryin out loud?*! Why don't they just say it like this: When you're out trolling in the Sesuit harbor in East Dennis it is suggested that to avoid snagging a depthfinder be used to indicate the depth of a fishing location. This should be mounted on your boat, just ahead of the steering wheel. At high water they'll be striking right in the wash, so swimming plugs could be the answer. Yet floating grass may continually foul your lures, so pull them directly past the nose of the rock lest the fish obstinately ignore your hardware only to swirl through pods of spearing.

If you're even more of a layman than that and you wanna know what to do besides dangle your line in the brine then just keep in mind that any fish'll bite if you got good bait and here's some of the very best: worms, bugs, flies (wet and dry), lures, plastic worms, insects, minnows, pieces of clam, bread, etc. And you catch them on: hooks. And the hooks are attached to: line. And the line gets weighed down by: sinkers. And you cast it out with: rod. And you reel it in by means of: reel. That's all you have to know and you can catch them bigger than life in any body of water in the world, even the most polluted, only certain species of fish need clean water. The ones that do are generally the tastiest fish in the world but you know what? Even the tastiest fish in the world tastes like shit so why bother eating when all the fun's in the catching? And don't forget: bring along the beer! Beer mixes with anything you can name and so does fishing: it's the only activitiy you don't have to be doing anything to do! So even if you can't attend a rock revival and at the same time climb a mountain with the Maharishi you can always fish for smallmouth and at the same time dance the polka. Fish'll be biting whether you're paying attention or not. You might even be fishing right now without knowing it! You might even be a regular Isaac Walton for all you know and it doesn't even depend on your eco-socionomic hooligomena. More people fish than play the banjo or milk a cow or vote for office, it's as universal as bowel activity on a foggy day.

There's all kindsa kulture just like all kinda kinks and you can't just sit in the front row and say "Gimme." That's only in general of course, like you can't be at a horse race and say "Gimme art appreciation, marijuana and a good movie," you have to go out and get each and every one of them by themselves. But you *can* go fishin any old time you want regardless of the circumstances. So you can go fish for all the other stuff that ain't there while you're doin what you're doin while you're doin somethin other than fishin. It might just happen to turn out you don't *catch* anything but at least you tried and a man's reach should exceed his grasp or what's a heaven for!

Okay, kounter-k'ers: get yer poles! It'll be kamouflage enough to make it look like you're doin somethin sides twiddlin your fingers and you might even hook a whopper and what's more: it's ezy!

# All Star Hi-Jinx

Gaylord Perry and his older bro Jim, it's not often that one family and one womb produces two brothers for the same all-star game, it might be one hundred million years before it happens again. But it might be every year pretty soon that the field looks like a basketball *court* even though it's a baseball *field*. That's caused by the new Cincinnati riverfront stadium where there was no breeze so the wind was not a factor in the all-star game because they have nothing but turf and lines on it to tell the infielders where to stand. Nixon threw out the first 2 balls like a girl and neither of them were used, not even for ping pong. The Commissioner's award for the biggest vote getter went to Hank Aaron who undoubtedly was the most popular of them all. There was only one winner for that unless of a tie but FOUR winners in the national pitch, throw, hit and slide competition including Bradley Grimmer, 9 yrs old, and Ted Williams (not *the*), 11 or 12. Speaking of 11 that's the number of Latin American countries who got the show over the international network. Dave Johnson made the American League squad by being an important cog—in the pennant drive of the Baltimore Birds—rather than a wheel. Richie Allen made it onto the National squad with his patented unusial (rhymes with Musial) swing like a buggy whip. But Dave Johnson had something *else* going for him too: ownership of the Golden Glove award for 2nd base, yes indeedy.

In inning number 2, 6 balls in a row were thrown by Jim Palmer. Multiply that by 5 and that's the number of wins Earl Weaver—incidentally the junior circuit skipper in addition to his duties with the Orioles—expects his Jim boy to win within exactly that number of yrs (5). During inning number 3 the fantastic scoreboard which can handle anything including cartoons said "WELCOME NBC" and Curt Gowdy said "Yes and we're happy to be here and it's gonna be a good one." *Gonna?* It was already the 3rd inning!

Johnny Bench went fishing for a bad pitch on 2-2 and was promptly returned to the dugout. It was 1 ball, 2 strikes to Frank Howard who is 6'7" and 275 with a very big question mark after that to anybody who's ever seen his midsection. Bunting may be a dying art with the new turf and managers will have to change their strategy, Luis Aparicio demonstrated *that* aptly. Too bad he wasn't in the National League or he would of been one of the many recipients of the familiar bugle call and charge that has become standard in the ball parks around America for the home team. Too bad the real hometowners left their hearing aids in the locker room cause the mighty Redlegs on the powerful senior circuit ball club didn't do half an ounce of old lint, charges or no. However the all-star game isn't everything, nor is it the whole season, nor does it count in the standings, nor does it change the batting averages or RBIs, nor does it cast anything bad about how good everybody was *up until* the big banana of them all, THE ALL-STAR GAME (there's only one a year now so it's as exclusive as a country club and only the cream of the cream are chosen so they gotta be good).

4 players were from Alabama, 6 from California, 4 from Texas and in all 22 states were represented and represented quite well I might add. Nobody disgraced his place of birth except maybe Roy White who rode the bench for the AL. Had he gotten in he could of employed himself well and proven that New York State deserves its place in the sun but like a lousy fool he didn't even get in. He could of gotten in by hitting 74 homers during the month of June but he did not. Why not? Because he wasn't good enough is why.

There was a tough call on a checked swing by Joe Morgan in the bottom of the 9th which could have meant curtains, instead it meant he got himself a hit because he stayed alive. Never give up is a motto worth following and nobody followed it as well as Joe, who kept alive the wonderfully thrilling rally which led to an extra-inning ball-o-rama when Pete Rose blew victory right then and there by swinging at the air 3 times running. Extra innings means they're beginning to run out of hot dogs, french fries, potato chips, soda, ham and cheese sandwiches and hot coffee and beer. But one thing they had no problem about running out of was Cheese Doodles by Old London, numero uno in the great big world of taste and crunch, because they didn't have any to begin with. They didn't have any, they didn't have any, that's that, period, nothing you can say. Those players who had acquitted themselves with honor on the playing field and were now resting their rumps in the dugout could sure have used a bag of these treats but unfortunately player comforts are still more neglected than ever.

The game stood tied 4 to 4 at the end of 10½, a good time for a win if there ever was one. Mrs. Joe Torre knew the time had come and even though she was wearing a tie over TV you could tell she was a woman and how can anyone concentrate on his hitting thinking about the likes of her while in the batter's box or the on deck circle? I'm speaking of Joe Torre, not about any other of the baseball profession because while others might of been thinking of her they didn't know from firsthand experience and that's what brings home the bacon so it was Joe Torre and Joe Torre only who was or wasn't ambivalent about pinch hit duty with victory in sight. But in the tenth and a halfth inning it was not to happen as it was one two three all down for the gallant NL.

Carl was called upon for defensive purposes to take over at first, Yastrzemski not Erskine. When you can do that it's either a sign you're versatile or that you've done it before. With this Carl it's a little of both since he knows infield nearly inside out due to having started his amazing career at shortstop. Understandably he had himself a double in the 12th, infield symmetry having been his trademark.

Finally the bottom of the 12th and finally Joe Torre took to the plate, his number 9 blaring off his massive back. 3 and 1 is what it was when he knocked the sphere towards infield great Brooks Robinson only to be tagged out by Carl himself on the way to first. What a frustrating evening for an avowed super star such as Joe! And with Clyde Wright in a sudden death situation with every pitch he threw, Joe was no soft touch yet he blew it. That in turn led to the excellent Clyde blowing it due to overconfidence leading to two hits in a row by Pete Rose and Billy Grabarkewitz and then somebody else to knock in Rose. And knock is just the word for it cause Rose knocked into Ray Fosse the great rough and tumble catcher for the AL on the way to getting a piece of plate with his right hand. Clyde and Ray lost the game, by the identical score of 5-4 that the NL won by. Remarkably the game had no goats so everybody went home and went to bed with a clear conscience. Many of the dreams that night were of baseball and the season ahead.

# Wiping for Pleasure

Planet Two-Ply Facial Tissue has a great wrapper but it's like rubber if you wanna use it on your ass and who needs two plys anyway? All you need two for is if you're afraid of getting any of the doody oody on your hands, if you are then two-ply is your ply. Other wipers only need one but which one?

The ads sure don't help out. Like how would anybody ever guess from the ad alone that Charmin is worth so much as a tryout in your own bathroom or lavatory? You'd probably rather go without dropping your load for a month rather than buy Charmin if there's nothing else in the store. But after all asswipe commercials have always believed in camouflage so in this case it's just a matter of *really* fuckin camouflaging the whole show, making you think the product is unworthy of purchase (or even use in somebody else's home). Cause it's *good paper* and possibly the first breakthru in the field since it began and don't just take my word for it, go out and give it a trial on your own seat!

Those ads also stress how squeezably soft the stuff is, well that's just pure cowshit: Planet is softer and so is Scott and so is Delsy! What a detour they're sending you on by even suggesting it's that soft! Cause what it's really good for is the way it operates on the roll. First it's the only commercial brand that has a loose end—no pun intended. The last sheet is unattached like it ain't with all other brands so you don't have to fumble with your fingers when you got some fast wipe-up to do. Also if you're pulling for some paper like your life depended on it chances are with any other brand it's gonna roll off the roll and hang down onto the floor and there's gonna be a real long lot of it in a pile at your feet and you can't reach that low so you'll have to either pull it up from the roll end or just rip it off and use the whole thing and that's probably too much so there won't be that much extra left at the end when you won't be able to get off the pot for a new roll. In other words that's what happens with every brand besides Charmin. But not with Charmin cause with Charmin what happens is it clings to the roll, the outside sheet always clings to the roll! It's got ridges is how and the ridges pick up a nice amount of shit too, nothing really out of the ordinary but the clinging business is what makes this a toilet essential from this day forth until death do us part. You GOTTA use it!

# 18 Feet or the IC4A?

It was either one or the other that was the dominant moment in a century's track and field, or should it really be called track *or* field? Or track and/or field? Well it was the Wildcats of Villanova who surged and finally sewed up the IC4A outdoor championship for the 10th time in 14 years (that's 168 long, lonely months) and it was C. W. Post (the corn flake people only they call them Post Toasties) emerging into second place with junior Ron Stonitsch finishing second to Villanova's Dicky Buerkle in the 3-mile RUN ( it wasn't a sprint, it wasn't a walk) but that's not the only reason it ended that way but almost. It was the 3,000-meter STEEPLECHASE what got won easily by Villanovan Des McCormack, a Roman Catholic through and thru from Dublin. Marty Liquori helped too with his 55.3 final lap to produce a 3:58.5 which was the icer on the icebox and V-I-C-T-O-R-Y for the rest of the boys back at school, all made possible by TRACK and not field. Andy O'Reilly in the 880 was another gold medal and another Roman too. Maryland—the land of Mary—finished second due to being field-conscious and overly secular, 2 strikes against them and it wasn't even stickball.

But field can certainly pay off to a field man even if not his team, particularly if the field man is a pole vaulter and his vault is over 18 feet. He not only gets the medal, he gets the record too, not the one on wax but the one on paper and the one in the hearts of his countrymen if he has a country. Christos Papanicolaou had both the country and the vault—and also the pole as well—when he ventured to clear 18 feet 1/4 inch in his homeland of Athens, Greece, a great place for philosophy and souvlaki and (American-sponsored military soldiers). Now there's another American sponsored in the land of Homer and ouzo, they sponsored his education at San Jose State, not only that but they MADE his pole (out of fiberglass) and set his sights high if you'll pardon the pun. Next thing you know they'll be pole vaulting up to the moon. It would save a lot of money but would probably equal out in terms of fiberglass research and all the money for vitamins and proteins they'd need to pump into the vaulter to make it all possible within this lifetime. And first they'd have to proceed slowly and break all the records in between, it's Zeno's paradox if they don't and Zeno was as Greek as Aristotle and the Aegean Sea. So they'd have to clear up the little matter of 18-2 1/4 which Papadopo or whatever his name is missed on his first, second and third attempts to better his own record. So even though he's a Greek he might not be the one for the project, in fact being Greek as he is and THE WAY HE BENDS THAT POLE might make him suspect anyway! But he deserves a try, he's only 28.

But if his name was Walter Rodenbaugh, R.J.C. Mitchell, Cornelius Warmerdam or John Uelses he'd be more memorable to stand the test of time as well as height. But time is all he's got, he's young.

# No Rocks in Roller

Rosetta Saunders got two, Rosetta Saunders got three, both at the Oakland Coliseum. Both? All three and all on the same jam and at the end of that one it was the SF Bay Bombers 43, the NE Braves 37. Then the Bombers got, no the Braves got three points back and it was 43-40. Increasing the lead is the thing to do. Joanie Weston moved up to reach the pack and she was thru but not quite and she was chewin her gum like a professional chewer and she got two and then Saunders was fixin to fight her (45-40). Both teams were down one skater for the next jam. Dorothy Lee number 25 for the Braves was in control, she was the only jammer out. For some reason she cut off the jam. O'Brien on the infield knocked Carol Meyer down. Punching and punching and punching, she got a one minute penalty and fell on her ass.

Eighth period saw the men out on the track. Larry Smith broke out and there was good blocking between Roman, Littles and Robinson. Bombers were rolling 46-40 and Ronnie Robinson the most valuable skater—and Ray Robinson's flesh and blood—was ready to go. Robinson and Littles made it work by tripping up O'Connell on a double block to knot it up 46-46. Fantastic skating led to Roman getting four and then he moved past McPherson for a fifth but only three were allowed. Why didn't the old grouches allow more? Wild play led to holding which dictated negating a couple and the penalty box for one minute and the fans were pissed.

The Braves outnumbered the Bombers 5 men to 4 and they pulled out all the stops to win this one. Tony Roman was out and moving and Robinson knew you don't catch Tony Roman so Ronnie cut it off after only two points and it was 49-49. Next jam Woodberry went after O'Connell with a knee and he drew the penalty and it was a good knee, the kind of knee people dream of. Man what action and 52-49 is the only way to describe it, it's just too fast to do anything but watch. It's faster than hockey, it's faster than squash, it's faster than Irish hurling.

Two minutes twelve to go and the action was so furious that the

Brave jammers couldn't even be picked out by the house announcer but officials counted five points. Robinson was strictly a blocker, he was not in scoring position. Bombers could not get by. Time ran out and they got two and it was tied. Which means girls come out for five minutes of sudden death and then the guys.

But the guys were needed no more than yesterday's fat swallowed marbles that have been spit up and thrown in the river. Or the bay, San Francisco Bay where the Bombers hail from. The gals won it for em 55-54. But the *way* they won it was the big show, they won it by only one point difference and it wasn't even basketball where that happens every month. And there isn't a ball in derby but as fate would have it there's something round in the way of a roller. If there was ice derby there wouldn't be anything round but there wouldn't be anything banked either, ice is impossible to bank unless it gets carved out by a sculptor and it would never be uniform unless there was a machine invented to do it and it would be a bitch to resurface during the breaks. So roller derby is supreme in team sports without a ball or a puck, it's supreme, it's supreme, it's supreme. And it's coed, and it's supreme.

Chris Hillman was never in the Supremes altho he's been in the Byrds and Burritos. One of his best pals is on the Bay Bombers but he's not saying who. That's the way roller derby friendships are. You can't let people know who it is or you might have to fear for your and his families. But Chris' buddy tells him that while occasionally you get derby which is phonus balonus in LA the matches in Northern California are honest to god pulverizers. Therefore the men gotta be men and the ladies gotta be ladies, what other sport can boast such guidelines for success?

They go around in circles, get it?

# Stay Away from Spitfire

Danny Fields was heard to say (don't tell John Sinclair he said this) that the High Energy Dee-troit Sounds are like their cars: buy one and two years later you'll be trading it in!! Well musically as well as automotively the only competition is from Queen Elizabeth II's homeland, makers of the worst tin lizzy with the lowest resale value ever to ride on high test: Spitfire.

A man must have his wheels if he's gonna move anything besides his bowels unless he uses his thumb. But it takes a thumb and forefinger to start a Spitfire engine unless you hold the keys in your clenched teeth and you might get your head caught in the steering wheel if you do: don't. Don't buy a Spitfire. If you know what's good for you. Don't rent one. If you know what's good for you. Axles break. Clutches give out. Speedometers don't work. Radiators leak. Fan belts break. Windshield wipers rot away. Mufflers last a week. Gas gauges don't last forever. Gas mileage starts okay but disappears out of sight. It may sound out of sight but it's not. The rear lights break every minute. The lenses and the bulbs. The license plate light retires if you lean on it. The turn signals have a mind of their own. The rims on the headlights fall off if you go over a bump. The front bumper is the only bumper. It's held on with saliva. Hence the name spitfire (also known as Sputfire). The locks on the doors get stuck. The trunks don't hold a medium size chicken. They leak. But only when there's rain. Causing pain. And rust. And mildew. If you lived in a Spitfire you'd get ill. Colds, tuberculosis, polio. Ruptured spine cause there's no room to sit. The headlights are often out of focus. The horn doesn't stay in but sometimes it stays on. Too long. And it's not loud enough to notify a pedestrian of impending doom. As if it could hurt a flood!

It's a weak car. It needs a ring job. The timing is atrocious. The spark plugs never spark. You're lucky if it starts. Even with a push. The jack won't lift a tack. Dealers are ruthless. They charge im-pus-ible prices for work. They come in colors hard to match with any known brands of paint. They have the ugliest hubcaps ever conceived. They won't run on regular. The top won't stay on in the wind. It rips when you're putting it on. It takes an hour or more. It won't keep out the cold. The plastic thing in the back becomes opaque in no time flat. They leak real bad in the back. If you can call it that. There's no room. The frame for the top stiffens between uses. When it gets opened up it cracks. You gotta buy a new one or forget about comfort. The mirror is a joke. The brakes don't do much. It swerves when you step down either hard or soft. The radio wire gets disconnected if you breathe. The antenna's as durable as a soda straw. So you can't hear Savoy Brown or Ten Years After. England stinx!

And don't try driving there in a Spogfire, it sinx.

# Wilcock's Selling His Mags

John Wilcock, one of the founders of the UPS and the *Village Voice* and the *East Village Other* and publisher of *Other Scenes* which used to get a free ride in Richard Neville's *Oz*, is selling his whole extensive enormous collection of underground memorabilia so he can get to Greece and live there til his number comes up which won't be for a while cause he's not that old. And even if he meets his mustard there's his wife Amber to worry about so buy some of his stuff won't you?

He's got two rooms just *full* of it, stuff like issues of *Other Scenes* and other issues of *Other Scenes* and other issues of *Other Scenes* too. And he's on every mailing list in the business and he gets just *cartons* and cartons of shit every day from outfits like the War Poland Society For Orphans and Cream Records. It's very vital stuff and somebody should buy it. But who? Certainly not the poor. Certainly not senior citizens, they wouldn't know what to make of it. Certainly not the family—Amber's brother Richard is a gym teacher at Clinton High—cause that would just be out of one pocket into another. But if Richard wants to visit them in Greece it might be a good idea for him to invest in their homestead by buying all the stuff and if there isn't room in the DeWitt Clinton gym he oughta give it to a library. If the library doesn't want it he should go to the store and trade them in for a complete set of John's five-dollar-a-day books, particularly *Greece on $5 a Day* if he intends to follow sis and brother-in-law to the dawn of Western Civilization.

But Richard better act fast now that John's in Japan or the UPSers'll be grabbing the stuff behind everybody's back and using it for toilet paper. They're using his office for office space right now and many of them don't wear underwear, for instance somebody named Melanie who's been fucking Jon Eisen for the last several weeks and Tom Forcade who wears a cowboy hat.

# Amusement Parkinson's

Gentlemen and gentlewomen gotta be amused and when they wanna be amused they go to a park, either nearby or far away. Sometimes they go *for* a park in which case it's usually nearby or the Mann Act gets brought in so they go nearby instead. Disneyland and Disney World ain't nearby if you're from America's heartland or the land of Rugomania but they're right around the corner if you're a dead gator from the Everglades or wherever it was they chopped all up for the building of Disney World, this only applies to Disney World, dead gators would still have a long way to go to get to Disneyland and they probably wouldn't be let in!

Dead gators can't have any fun but people can and when they wanna have fun while being amused they go to the fun house, all amusement parks have them but they're not much fun anymore, and animal lovers never get to run them and they should. They should open a fun house where they have rabid dogs running around, no leashes for these babies! A human would walk in there after paying his 35¢ for some fun, 70¢ if it's him and his date. The place would be entirely 100% dark and the sounds of barks would seem like the usual harem-scarem, nothing unusual so the man and his companion would proceed further in. Hot breath will mingle with the barks as Jojo wanders further into the darkness and—then—ka-chow! Jaws close and saliva flows into bloodstreams inoculated against tetanus but not the dread HYDROPHOBIA!

Should they get their horribly painful shots in the belly free on the (fun) house from Disney World after they get bit? Well it *is* the legal liability of Disney's heirs but they've reneged on their liabilities before. Yet there is a moral liability which goes above and beyond the legal one so shots should be given absolutely free. Painlessness is man's birthright too and so there should be novocain first so it doesn't hurt as much.

If the experiment works for the Disney parks it could then be brought over to several others like Berry Park, Palisades Park, Freedomland, Tokyo's Benvenuti Stadium and Playland in Falls River.

# Neil Sedaka: Horseman of the Apocalypse

Neil Sedaka's buying a horse for his cousin Arnold Sedaca with a c who goes to grad school in math at Yale, quite a horseman in his own right. You can bet your eye teeth he's gonna make sure the equine has its full complement of parts, including poll, forehead, face, muzzle, throat-latch, windpipe, jugular-groove, shoulder, point of shoulder, chest, arm (horses have an arm too), forearm, knee, fetlock, pastern, cannon, seat of splint, elbow, flank, stifle, cannon, hock, goskin, quarter, thigh, hip-joint, croup, hip, coupling, loins, back, withers, crest and neck. Being from Missouri, both him and Arnold know the value of a good set of goskins and so it goes for their music and math and their own set of anatomical equipment. Particularly the voice box and the pencil fingers and the feet (they both stand when they work, always).

Neil was always the most popular singer of all time and now he's back with his new phonograph album on the Kirshner label called *Emergence*. As far as he goes on the album, he's, um, he's Neil Sedaka, Neil Sedaka is, he, ull, uhh, hmm, uh he uhh, it's in fact, as a matter of fact, factually speaking he, he, yes he's, you could say that, how about the, the, if, and, the album is, as albums go, fact of the matter, is, it's that, um, um, ha, it's, whulps, a, hmm, huh, yes Neil Sedak, Neil Sedaka, Sedaka that's right, here's what he is, he's, oops, an old sailor once said, he said and it applies here because he's, because, on account of, therefore, he a, oops a mighty, ubg, unh, uh huh, yeah, you got it, it's, and it's but, buh, ah, a, uhm, ooh, oo-wee, whew, sheesus, afraid so, um and, hoo, gimme, huh huh huhhuh, wupp, whoa, heck he is, but it's true, heck, can't deny, y'know, yuh, mmm, huck, humma, gotcha, uh, a, he's, just him, by himself, he's, you'll have to agree, you will, yes sir, yes siree Bob, buh, an, an, and a, what's the word, yeah he, uh, he, Neil Sedaka's, is, whatsa, he's, um, swell and so's the album and let's hope it sells a lot even without any promotion. We can start the ball rolling by spreading the word by word of mouth. I'm telling you, now you tell somebody else and maybe even a few somebody elses and they'll tell somebody else too and it's gonna snowball and Neil'll have his first gold record since "Breaking Up Is Hard to Do" and "Ghost Riders in the Sky."

# Caging Animals like They Was Animals

There's this show called *Lancelot* (not the missing) *Link* where they let the chimps wander around with clothes on saying funny things just like they was non-subhumans. They're even allowed to pilot aeroplanes and drop heavy rocks into the pool for a guaranteed big splash. But as anthropomorphic as it gets *they don't have the chimps' names on the credits at the end of the show* and even the hairdo doopers get a mention just cause they're higher primates! Fair?

There's this likable fellow named Boots, family name Schwartzcohen, and pets are his forte and he keeps them in his fort, his not-very-spacious urban dwelling. Urban dwellings are cages and so he's caged too and so it's a matter of how much room in the cage he wants to offer his sub-mammalian cage partners. And his decision so far has been *not very much* thank you!

So there's a fine specimen of a soft-shell turtle in a tank too small for a six-pack of half-quarts and he has his snout sticking out the opening looking for a friend with his fishy eyes, nice feet on him too and all he can do with them is swim his way into the glass in pursuit of Lake Erie. The water in there's cleaner than Erie but the companionship ain't. But of course he's got Boots and Boots has his matamata too and it's a good thing the matamata has Boots cause he sure don't have that much lebensraum s'il vous plaît! Can't even turn around and the only thing turtles in nature ain't able to do is turn over (if they're on their back): a sin and a crime against nature. And G-d never intended fuckin iguanas to live four to a cage cause if He did He wouldn't of put them in Mexico where there are no cages: four in a cage and one of em's a young'un so he's gonna be livin the blues cage-un style for purty close to an iguana lifetime, poor puppy!

But strangely he owns no mammals but that must be cause they make more overt spatial demands and their shitting calls for walking and cleaning unlike with the birds in Boots's ungilded cage with the roaches crawling in and out at will. Boots has spoken out against his roaches and he doesn't even consider them his, well *lucky for them* hoop oop ee doo! But he don't like them mostly cause of their relative free-dum and he's no dummy but he is kinda dumb about all the mice running round and he makes believe he doesn't notice em, wotta liar!

But he ain't lyin when he says he don't know the sex of his tarantula, cause he don't. Should he? Yes. Cause tarantula owners should know the sex of their tarantulas. But at least the arachnid's got the biggest dwelling per body unit in the whole place (cause the previous dweller bought a farm when Boots's better half destroyed the whole place cause she thought he was payin more attention to the animules than her, he's the guy who wrote the beloved "Tuffy the Tuna" and he loves his bipeds, quadrupeds and octopeds even more that tuna but—says he—not more than the fair sex) but the top's screened over and the roaches can't get in, and as everybody knows tarantulas love roaches. No they don't love them in the sexual sense, they just love to eat them.

But along with the shelter and food (animals except for TV chimps don't need clothing—those lucky fucks!) Boots's little pals have some swell scenery to remind them of their home long ago—unless they were born in a pet store, but most non-plants aren't. There are trees and pebbles to keep their nostalgia ripe so they can lead healthy, active lives but they never get to see their parents and have no visiting hours except at Boots's discretion. The iguanas never even get to stroll around the joint cause Boots is too slow for em, the old slowpoke!

FREE ALL ANIMAL PRISONERS! POWER TO THE PACHYDERMS!

# Kike Cods and Big Lemons

Geez! Lemons are *everywhere* these days, even in toilet bowl remedies and in the ad this guy who's sailing the boat in the toilet tank throws her a lemon. There even used to be an ad when they were still doing cigarettes on TV where the purchaser goes up to the candy stand and asks the guy "Is there a lemon cigarette?" Not even "Do you have a lemon cigarette?" Well the answer was no on both counts but it could easily have been yessiree. There's just lemons everywhere and Malcolm Durand the writer wrote a book called *Kike Cunt and Big Lemons* but the publishers made him change it. The lemon part was okay but they figured the cunt part would disqualify it from distribution and sales and that's always the name of the game. They didn't like the kike part either on the grounds that it was anti-semitic but many books have appeared in print with nigger and wop-a-dago somewhere in the title so there should have been no trouble over kike and they should have let him call his book *Kike Cod and Big Lemons* if he wanted.

But he did not want. Instead he did a hatchet job on the title and came up with *Schav and Shaft*. Here's how it works. Schav is the flavor of pussy, that's what it actually tastes like, it doesn't taste like fish as many millions have been led to believe. And shaft is because lemons could either be the two balls or also the stuff that's in them tastes slightly sour and slightly salty (and salt goes along with lemons when you're drinking tequila) and lemons are sour and it all comes out of the open end of the shaft. But he could have called it *Kike Cod and Big Lemons* or—if he wanted to be honest about the flavor and avoid remarks from the JDL—he could have renamed it *Cool Cud and Big Lemons*.

Lemon's important in literature as in household items but not in all cases. One case is the case of Borden's lemon yogurt. Now it's an okay thing for the rest of those Swiss-style yogos to be on the pasty side. The paste means it's homogenized and that way you don't gotta stir it up to get the fruit all around. The fruit in

Dannon's and Breakstone's and Lacto is at the bottom and it's either juicy or it's gooey. Now lemon is good when it's juicy and it's also good when it's gooey, if you've ever et one of those Drake's pies or Mrs. Wagner's you'll heartily agree. But *lemon paste*?!

It's unheard of. It stinks. Don't eat it or you'll lose your faith in lemons.

# Cause and Effect

(212) 757-9940 is the number that was posted for calling at the Sickle Cell Anemia Telethon but some guys came down in person to pay their dues. Some were short and some were tall. Among the latter was over-30 Dick Barnett with his 500 bucks to slap into Nipsey Russell's eager palm just like it was a basket about waist-high. But there was no hole at the bottom, baskets wouldn't have them either if they wanted to save the balls that came their way. Baskets are incredibly stupid because balls can bring anywhere from 5 dollars on up on the open market and they sure can bounce. So do checks but not Dick's and then he got his chance to utter something special into the mike of very importance. And it was to the effect that he hoped his appearance in person on stage would "have an effect on the cause." (Or did he say *affect*?)

And the cause was those sickles that build up and get thick and mean inside the bloodstream of certain individuals unlucky enough to have been born before the advent of sickle cell anemia telethons but now they have them and Peaches and Herb were on hand and Betty Shabazz too with her healthy head of hair straight as a pipe. And the camera work was oh so fine like when they had the Voices of East Harlem in the spotlight and they told them to play until the sickle cell anemia girl's can was all filled up with contributions they didn't show much of the piano guy. And is there any reason they should've? No because pianos use ivory which comes from dead elephants which have to be alive in order to be useful in sickle cell research. Any elephants born during the course of the show were still virtual youngsters at the conclusion cause it only lasted 4 hrs. No it was 4 and a half.

And the last half hour was the best all nite, that was when they brought on the mountain climber who told about how he first found out about having the sickle cell trait—not the disease, just the trait—when he got on top of Pike's Peak and felt excruciating pains in his stomach and chest. He thought it was a heart attack but was relieved to find out it was just because of less oxygen at that altitude which the sickle cells had something to do with in a *deleterious way.* But what's actually worse, a bad pump or bad pump fluid? Bad pump fluid because there's more of it in the body.

But some unanswered questions remain, like who did song-stress Jean Dushann think she was jiving with that lame-ass soul-stirring rendition of "For Once in My Life"? The honks with the bread out in audience land? The laugh-hungry brothers and sisters in the theater? Others?

# Finis

Now it's *your* turn to write a chapter and it's the last one so you get the last laff. As you all know "he who laffs last laffs the best" so you're bound to be one up on me. The words of this finale have already been written for you and they're listed in alphabetical order, all you gotta do is just put em back in sequence and the numeral *following* the word indicates what the desired sequence is. Like if it says 3 it's the third word and 55 is the 55th, you don't have to follow orders but you get court martialed by the Book Brigade if you don't. It's not an easy task and it's not gonna go fast but good things don't come easy altho they do come in small packages. And they're worth waiting for but don't mind me if I don't sit around and wait for you. Okay, on your mark, get set....GO:

1.  a 3
2.  a 55
3.  a 60
4.  a 63
5.  a 83
6.  all 107
7.  also 7
8.  And 37
9.  and 10
10. and 13
11. and 44
12. and 62
13. and 65
14. and 74
15. and 82
16. and 92
17. and 108
18. and 140
19. apricot, 32
20. are 146

21. at 106
22. be 112
23. blueberry, 34
24. boysenberry, 35
25. But 48
26. But 123
27. But 151
28. but 5
29. call 51
30. called 117
31. can 98
32. can't 76
33. ch 64
34. cherry 23
35. (cherry, 16
36. cluster 137
37. coffee, 31
38. consonants. 141
39. counter-culture 43
40. cranberry 27
41. Culture 1
42. culture 9
43. culture 41
44. culture 46
45. cultured 11
46. cultured 14
47. disguise 77
48. dogsweat. 86
49. don't 152
50. e 68
51. even 109
52. even 131
53. everywhere 148
54. exceptions 147
55. extra 135
56. eyestrain! 159
57. frills 81
58. forget 100
59. fucking 125
60. fun 105

# About the Author

Meltzer grew up in Rockaway, a sleazy beach community, hated the beach by age 5. Boyhood favorites: Buster Crabbe and Guy Madison. Didn't do much except read boxing magazines until college, where he starred as the coxswain of the crew. Chummed around with happenings innovator Allan Kaprow and created Meltzer's Clothing Store, four tons of clothing in a room the size of your closet, Stony Brook 1965. Did a Meltzer's Comic Book Show the summer of '66 in a refrigerator storeroom in the Bronx but the art from that proved too heavy to be carried around so he abandoned the visual stuff for writing, going on to invent rock criticism in no time flat. Resurrected an old manuscript called *The Aesthetics of Rock* (originally written '64-'65) and revised it to produce the earth-shattering opus of the same name, published in 1970. Many more books in the can, including *Soft Dull* (sports) and *Secret Cigareen* (TV). Currently working on the great braille novel, to be published only in braille so that non-braille readers will just have to learn it if they feel like reading it. Doesn't read himself, feels it hurts the eyes immeasurably. Doesn't really care much for writing either, does it because it's easier than plumbing. Has written for virtually every rag in the underground field. Writes lyrics for the Blue Oyster Cult and sang with them briefly when they were the Soft White Underbelly. Made a couple of movies, taught an aesthetics class in Baltimore (1967) for middle-aged teachers coming back to get a masters, made them eat watermelon in front of the room (Margaret Mead's niece was in the class and all she talked about was pygmies).

"Well I do these dead animals in jello, I find em dead and I stick em in a Tropicana orange juice bottle and fill it up with jello, I have seven of em in my refrigerator right now including two stillborn kittens in lemon and orange respectively.

"I once got dead drunk 14 days running and some L A woman told me that even Jim Morrison—a former intimate acquaintance of hers—hadn't ever done it that many days running and that wasn't even the end of it.

"I have what has to be the largest collection of bottle caps (oh about 4000 all different) among living American writers, who has a bigger one?"—R. Meltzer

# More About the Author

All quotes this time? OK:

"Since *Gulcher* I've been doing the same basic shit, writing 10-11-12-13 hours a day, 365 per, annum after annum... a miserable, unrewarding chore I wouldn't wish on a dog. Exceptions: led (and sang with) not really horrible punk band Vom (as Mr. Vom), '77–'78; all-night punkrock deejay, KPFK (fired for using cusswords on mike), '79–'81.

"I haven't gone bald yet (or even gray). My vision and blood pressure are a joke—two jokes—but my arthritis seems under control. Wrote the lyrics to Blue Oyster Cult's 'Burnin' for You,' for which I'm still owed $12,000, more (by four large figures) than the mean annual income for all the growed-up years of my life.

"Bookwise, let's see, *Soft Dull* never came out (company folded). *Secret Cigareen* was only a bluff, no such book, but the title's too good to dump (& should resurface). An even better title, and possibly my best bk., is *17 Insects Can Die in Your Heart*, a collection of verse from '83 containing no poem with such title (or even w/ that line in it). *Tropic of Nipples*, more fine pomes, is due out in the early to mid '90s. Already out, gone, remaindered: first two volumes of *Caned Out*, my fabulous 'rediscovered' 1970 autobio; *L.A. Is the Capital of Kansas*, another hot one with a full sentence f'r title; *Richard Meltzer's Guide to the Ugliest Buildings of Los Angeles*, a thrilling treatise on, uh, I don't remember. And other shit—look it up. (Currently at work on a so-called novel.)

"I live in L.A. and hate every minute of it. Would rather clean tires with my tongue than write screenplays. Haven't taught *dick* in twenty-three years but would love to teach a course in the writings of Faulkner, Kerouac, Melville and/or myself—won't somebody ask me?

"When I turned forty I played alto sax awhile, or tried (and might try again). As of May '90 I've been on *Joe Franklin* three times, four counting radio. I haven't been 'R.' Meltzer since '75 and no longer collect bottle caps. Haven't smoked a cigar in five

years—one more will give me cancer. Current hobby: laundry.
Should I mention my used tampon sculptures?"

Richard Meltzer
Los Angeles
April, 1990

# More About This Dizzy Book

A couple months ago, filling out my Citadel author question-naire, in response to "Please write 75 to 100 words on the book's theme, intent and underlying concept," like a good little boy I scribbled the following:

> When I first wrote the damn thing, in the summer-fall (I believe) of '71, rock criticism, while still in its infancy, had already become as big a whore, a cripple, a mocker of truths both emotional and factual, as any marketplace-tied "critical" genre that had come before. My own program ("mission") *as* a rockwriter, one scrupulously ignored or avoided by virtually all others, was to sys-tematically disassemble—*deconstruct*, ha, as it were—the monster/mess I'd played such a passionate role in helping create in the first place (and which, 1990, is still with us, more loathsome than ever, with us unfortunately *forever*). With this book I focused my deconstructive rage and rigor on not only rock-critical thought and behavior but on various related (and unrelated) genres of etcetera ("countercultural" and otherwise), and in the process managed to pull off (luck into??) a landmark of Ameri-postmodernist ya ya ya. Propelled by *classic* torrents of "automatic critical prose," its most enduring subtext is the screaming need for punk-rock, for *a* punk-rock (well before the fact).

What horseshit, right? But that was before I'd actually read the fucker, reread it, for the first time in 18-19 years. Having just right now done so, jeez, I can't begin to tell you how AMAZED I was, am, by the goddam *ferocity* of the "deconstruction"—demolition's more like it. The kitchen sink, dad: destroy all discourse! Song, singer, singin'—all down in flames. Coherence, even euphony, tension/release, cadence, have no place, certainly no "privileged" place, in this prose. "Sounds good," "reads good"—a pair of quaint, disposable bourgeois notions (disposed with).

Some of it reads so clunky I just wanna kick it. Line after line of "intentional bad writing" (believe me) that isn't even *good* bad writing, it's just bad. Too many *and*'s, *so*'s, *even*'s, *the*'s, *that*'s, *too*'s extraneous whatsems only there because they *were* extraneous: someone, evidently, was looking to *fill pages* or something. All these ridiculous exclamation points—gee how *bombastic*. The expression "beat his ass" 93 times. Reading this trash now, meticulous frigging professional that I've become, I feel like the final Flying Wallenda, whatever his name was, on his final ropewalk over that plaza, the time the wind blew him off. Still holding his pole, halfway down he clutched it to his chest, the final reflexive act, and here I go wincing, kicking and (just as reflexively) writing this pointless afterword—nothing of import I can do to break *my* fall either. (I still use no net.) How can I let them reprint this shit?

Then I remember—thank fuck for something—that what it was about was KINDERGARTEN. Kindergarten, y'know, pre-school, as sacred writerly First Principle: everybody, I contended (and still contend), should go play with mud for a while, fishtank slime, at least blocks. Stack 'em, knock 'em over (piss on 'em). Splash paint on teacher's pantsuit. Throw spitballs. Every growed-up writeperson, every so-called creative jackjill (of whatever persuasion), really *should* get that "basic"—or why bother?— am I right? Well, I can't think of too many fellow writers, "Counterculture Era," who actually went and did it—Nick Tosches and a handful of fanziners; S. Clay Wilson and Rory Hayes if you count comix—which in all fortuity has left *Gulcher* as our sole surviving bulk record of what this sort of number (made print) might even have looked like. Truly *infantile* (the Fount of It All) it probably ain't, but you can't have everything. (Usually you can't have anything.) Likewise, my bull-in-a-china-shop antics seem at times too bull-lame, bull-immature, bull-leisurely, stopping short of total devastation, or even bona fide *devastation*\*—remember, this was play, not work.

---

\*For a bulk sample of my *mature* devastation, see *The Outside Dope*—well you can't see it—a '74 sports book (writ for Scribners, no less) which has yet to be published.

And *what* play, christ, what joy! THIS, if anything, is what I right this sec feel mega-nostalgia for, far more than for rocknroll, which in any event had been dead, gone, g'bye long before *Rolling Stone* deigned to found (and briefly fund) Straight Arrow. (Lester to the contrary, this *is* a post-rock book, I wouldn't shit you.) Boy oh *boy* do I wish I could still write this way, one draft with malice, mangling syntax, mixing metaphors, sprinting down the page and not caring beans whether pages/filled were "good pages" or "bad pages," caring even less whether in the process I'd actually "said anything" (if it ain't said in real time, real *writer* time, what could it possibly mean to say it?), least of all whether every damn syllable had been in place—this was *prose*, man (not poetry!), laid down like easy miles of asphalt. Which is not to say I *would* write this way, not at the expense of all sorts of grim, solemn, writenose-to-the-grindstone middle age claptrap, not unless, that is, you could turn it on/off like a faucet, which of course you can't (required—hey—is a full-life commitment to *total* play, total mischief), but it's nice, I guess, to know that I once wrote this way, that I once (at the grindstone) had "fun."

Fun, sure, Lester was right about that much—but "humanist"? "Interested in absolutely everything"? Sorry, dead guy, and sorry you never made it to middle age like I have, but the one key flavor you seem to have missed in *Gulcher* is its CONTEMPT. Contempt for, well, the cultural kitchen sink (and nearly all its plumbing). The goodtime Lester, especially early, had a blind spot for such biz, though we always buzzed a shared contempt for that canon of Alternate Fascism, the smarmy notion of "hip." If for *any reason* you suspect the book, through no fault of its own, of having picked up a crust of hip cooties like so many barnacles, please burn it, stab it, wipe your hind parts with it, or feed it to goats. Please!

Richard Meltzer
*Bastille Day, 1990*

**CITADEL UN DERGROUND**

CITADEL UNDERGROUND provides a voice to writers whose ideas and styles veer from convention. The series is dedicated to bringing back into print lost classics and to publishing new works that explore pathbreaking and iconoclastic personal, social, literary, musical, consciousness, political, dramatic and rhetorical styles.

Take Back Your Mind

For more information, please write to:

CITADEL UNDERGROUND
Carol Publishing Group
600 Madison Avenue
New York, New York 10022